ETHICS IN PUBLIC AND COMMUNITY HEALTH

Edited by Peter Bradley and Amanda Burls

London and New York

First published 2000
by Routledge
11 New Fetter Lane, London EC4P 4EE

Simultaneously published in the USA and Canada
by Routledge
29 West 35th Street, New York, NY 10001

Routledge is an imprint of the Taylor & Francis Group

© 1999 selection and editorial matter Dr Peter Bradley and
Dr Amanda Burls; individual contributions, the contributors

Typeset in Times by BC Typesetting, Bristol
Printed and bound in Great Britian by
TJ International Ltd, Padstow, Cornwall

British Library Cataloguing in Publication Data
A catalogue record for this book is available from the British Library

Library of Congress Cataloging in Publication Data
Ethics in public and community health/edited by Peter Bradley
and Amanda Burls.
p.   cm. – (Professional ethics)
Includes bibliographical references and index.
1. Public health–Moral and ethical aspects.   2. Community health
services–Moral and ethical aspects.   3. Medical ethics.
I. Bradley, Peter, 1965– .   II. Burls, Amanda, 1954– .
III. Series.
RA652.E886   1999
174'.2–dc21   99-29709
                                                                                  CIP

ISBN 0–415–22054–8 (hbk)
ISBN 0–415–22055–6 (pbk)

PROFESSIONAL ETHICS
General editor: Ruth Chadwick
Centre for Professional Ethics, University of Central Lancashire

Professionalism is a subject of interest to academics, the general public and would-be professional groups. Traditional ideas of professions and professional conduct have been challenged by recent social, political and technological changes. One result has been the development for almost every profession of an ethical code of conduct which attempts to formalise its values and standards. These codes of conduct raise a number of questions about the status of a 'profession' and the consequent moral implications for behaviour. This series seeks to examine these questions both critically and constructively. Individual volumes will consider issues relevant to particular professions, including nursing, genetic counselling, journalism, business, the food industry and law. Other volumes will address issues relevant to all professional groups such as the function and value of a code of ethics and the demand of confidentiality.

Also available in this series:

CONTENTS

CONTRIBUTORS

John Beal, Senior Registrar in Dental Public Health, Leeds Health Authority.

Peter Bradley, Consultant in Public Health Medicine, Institute of Public Health, Oslo, Norway.

Joanna Breach, Ex-lecturer in Dental Public Health, Department of Transcultural Oral Health, Eastmann Institute, London.

Amanda Burls, Senior Lecturer in Public Health Medicine, University of Birmingham.

Juan Cabello-López, Cardiologist and Clinical Epidemiologist, Director of Unidad de Investigación, Hospital General Universitario de Alicante, Spain.

Corinne Camilleri-Ferrante, Director, Anglia Clinical Audit and Effectiveness Team, Institute of Public Health, Cambridge.

Henrietta Ewart, Consultant in Public Health Medicine, Northamptonshire Health Authority.

Siân Griffiths, Director in Public Health Medicine, Oxfordshire Health Authority.

Homa Hasan, Genetic counsellor and researcher, Centre for Medical Ethics, University of Oslo.

Ruth Holt, Senior Lecturer in Dental Public Health, Department of Transcultural Oral Health, Eastmann Institute, London.

Louise Locock, Research Associate, Templeton College, University of Oxford.

Nigel Monaghan, Consultant in Dental Public Health, Bro Taf Health Authority.

Gill Needham, Subject Information Specialist (Team Leader), Open University, Milton Keynes.

Jan Helge Solbakk, Professor of Medical Ethics, University of Oslo.

Sarah Stewart-Brown, Director of Health Services Research Unit, Department of Public Health, University of Oxford.

Pat Troop, Director of Public Health Medicine, NHS Executive Eastern, Milton Keynes.

PREFACE

This book is concerned with the ethical issues in public and community health. The purpose of these specialities is to improve the health of populations or groups rather than concentrating on individuals. Much of the ethical debate in health care has concentrated on the interaction between health-care worker and patient, but very little has been written about an ethical attitude to the population as a whole. We hope that this book will begin to redress the balance.

The topics chosen – prioritisation, screening, public participation, and health promotion – reflect current practice in international public health. They are the sites of the major ethical issues: What health services should be available? Who should have access to which health services? What are the best strategies for preventing disease? How can professional and public views be reconciled? When can an individual's health needs override the choice of a community?

We have tried to answer these questions by recourse to ethical theory and practical examples in public health practice. The chapters include the results of ethical research, systematic reviews and the application of ethical theory to real situations, both in the UK and abroad.

Peter Bradley
Amanda Burls

SERIES EDITORS' PREFACE

Professional Ethics is now acknowledged as a field of study in its own right. Much of its recent development has resulted from rethinking traditional medical ethics in the light of new moral problems arising out of advances in medical science and technology. Applied philosophers, ethicists and lawyers have devoted considerable energy to exploring the dilemmas emerging from modern health-care practices and their effects on the practitioner–patient relationship.

Beyond health care, other groups are beginning to think critically about the kind of service they offer and about the nature of the relationship between provider and recipient. In many areas of life social, political and technological changes have challenged traditional ideas of practice.

Even in health care, however, ethical dilemmas are not confined to health care professionals and their relationships with individual patients. Although public health ethics has been relatively neglected in traditional medical ethics, it includes a number of complex ethical issues, such as criteria for population screening (including genetic screening), the increasing demands on health care resources, and ongoing debates about freedom of choice versus public good in the context of vaccination or water fluoridation.

The editors have organised the essays into three sections, dealing with prioritisation, screening, and public participation and health promotion. The volume seeks to address both the applicability of ethical frameworks and the phenomena of current practice. A prominent theme is the importance of attending to the process of decision-making, in addition to theoretical frameworks.

The Professional Ethics book series seeks to examine ethical issues in the professions and related areas both critically and constructively. Some volumes address issues relevant to all professional groups, such as the nature of a profession. Other volumes examine issues relevant to particular professions, including those which have hitherto received little attention, such as health care management, general practice and genetic counselling.

Part I

RATIONING AND PRIORITISATION

In this section of the book the ethical issues of rationing and prioritisation are discussed. Prioritisation resulting from limited resources inevitably leads to ethical dilemmas; for example, if one group receives health care then another may be denied it. As public health practice concerns itself with maintaining health in the whole population, the issue is particularly pressing.

Traditionally priorities have been decided implicitly, at the point of making a clinical decision or by governmental resource allocation. In some countries this process is becoming more explicit as a result of the reforms of the health care system. For example in the UK health authorities now have a direct input into decisions about whether a treatment is available or what groups of people receive certain kinds of health care. This process might take into account national priorities, the views of local professionals, the views of the public and evidence of clinical effectiveness of treatments. The level of public participation in deciding priorities is extremely varied.

In the first chapter by Bradley, the case for a move to a more explicit process is considered. Some of the ethical frameworks which could support decision-making are presented. However, he concludes that although useful, the theories only offer a partial solution to the practicalities of decision-making. The theme of the importance of the process of decision-making is considered in other sections of the book, especially Part III, where the relevance of public participation is considered.

The second chapter, by Ewart, describes an implicit decision-making process for the funding by a health authority of extra-contractual referrals. The emphasis in this case was on developing an ethical framework by local consensus. Griffiths's chapter, in contrast, shows the need for explicitness in decision-making as made possible in a Priorties Forum. Even so, this process has very limited public participation. In the chapter by Needham, a process for full participation by the public is described. The logistic, practical and ethical problems of getting decisions made by the public accepted by health authorities are discussed. Another way of sharing decision-making is discussed by Locock in her chapter comparing international attempts at priority-setting. The ethical bases for these processes are discussed. All these processes achieve only partial solutions to the dilemmas of prioritisation in health care. Prescriptive rationing criteria, as used in Oregon, for example, are seen to be too inflexible. Loose criteria, as used in New Zealand, are not seen to carry enough force to influence decisions. However, cultural, ethical and other factors do influence the choices made in each health care system.

In conclusion, there are no *easy* solutions to deciding which ethical frameworks or which processes will help to resolve prioritisation dilemmas. The different chapters illustrate a variety of approaches.

1

APPLICATION OF ETHICAL THEORY TO RATIONING IN HEALTH CARE IN THE UK: A MOVE TO MORE EXPLICIT PRINCIPLES?

Peter Bradley

Introduction

At present, rationing policy in the UK National Health Service (NHS) is mostly implicit in that decisions about which treatments should be funded are decided without national or local debate. Many believe that a more explicit and open debate on rationing policy is inevitable. Presently, decisions about health care rationing are often inconsistent and judgements unclear. Consideration of the ethical principles that lie behind health care decision-making can help decision-makers realise which values underpin their decisions and where their judgements are inconsistent. This chapter summarises the arguments used in ethical theory and the implications of having certain philosophical frameworks in health care rationing.

A definition of rationing

The term 'rationing' is often replaced by phrases relating to resource allocation or priority-setting. Although the terms are used in slightly different ways, they all arise from a similar assumption, that is, it is impossible to meet all the health care demands from the population within the NHS on current levels of public expenditure.[1]

Rationing of health care services can be defined as: 'an explicit or implicit policy to withhold specific measures of treatment or care on the grounds that their economic costs are prohibitive'.[2] In other words, rationing of health care may mean that a specific treatment or type of care is denied to a group of people or to an individual, even if that treatment would confer health benefit to them.

Is rationing a necessity?

The rationing debate has intensified in the last few years because of a perceived funding crisis in the NHS. This is attributed to several factors. For example, the population of the UK is ageing, and traditionally elderly people have used the resources of the NHS more heavily than other age groups. There has been an increase in the use of high technology in the NHS, making many more treatments available than before and, more often than not making treatment more expensive. Public expectations of and demands upon the health service have grown in the last few decades.[3] Total NHS funding increased by 105 per cent between 1980/1 and 1989/90.[4] Even allowing for inflation, this is an enormous increase.

Some have argued that rationing would be an unnecessary policy if the NHS were 'more appropriately' funded,[5] for example, by diverting resources to health from other government ministries. However, in this chapter, we will assume that the budget for health is unlikely to meet all health demands. The NHS is, at present, largely funded through public rather than private means, and the source of this public funding is mainly taxation.[6] At the present level of funding, the NHS cannot satisfy the current demand for health care services.[7] Several authors believe that some sort of health care rationing is inevitable.[8]

Types of rationing in the NHS

Rationing takes many forms in the NHS. It is done by restricting the budget for health at the level of *governmental ministries*,[9] or by *geographical areas* using resource allocation formulae,[10] or for *certain types of health care services*, for example community health services. Other types of rationing include restricting the *number of people* who might receive a particular treatment, for example denying expensive heart operations to smokers or the elderly.[11] *Access to treatments* can be limited by *waiting lists*, by the health authority's or the doctor's *ability to pay*, by *age limits*, or by the *number of treatments* available (such as assisted fertility services).[12]

Where rationing occurs in the NHS, decisions are usually made without public knowledge or involvement,[13] either by individual clinicians (when a doctor denies a patient treatment);[14] or centrally, through the amount of funds given to each health authority or purchaser.[15] So rationing decisions are usually implicit. There is a continuing misconception that the NHS is always able to deliver services according to health care need, so if a patient 'needs' treatment, economic reasons will not preclude it.[16]

Occasionally, decisions have been more explicit. There have been a number of high profile cases about the rationing of resources by purchasers, such as the case of child B, diagnosed with leukaemia and denied specialist treatment on the NHS[17] and the debate over the use of β interferon in the treatment of multiple sclerosis.[18] Some health authorities have produced lists of specific treatments that they are not prepared to fund.[19]

Despite this, the general consensus seems to be that rationing in the NHS continues to be mainly unadmitted.[20] But it seems inevitable health care costs will rise and demands from the population will continue to increase. Health inequality between social groups is also increasing.[21] As public concern grows about the limitations of the health service, implicit decision-making by a minority may become unacceptable. The decision-making process behind health care rationing decisions will need to become more open to view and the public more informed.

How might rationing decisions be made in the UK?

Many groups *could* be involved in future rationing decisions,[22] for instance the medical profession, health authorities, primary care groups, certain sections of the public, central government, expert committees and the courts.[23] More open debate is now being encouraged in the NHS.[24] However, this approach will only be useful if all parties are appropriately informed in the issues related to health care rationing.[25] Previous explicit approaches have shown that public and professional views are likely to be at variance.[26] Such a situation was encountered in the state of Oregon, USA, which used public opinion to inform health policy. Apart from recognised difficulties in the consultation process, some of the conclusions reached by public consultation were unacceptable to politicians and professionals. For example, the treatment of crooked teeth had higher priority than the management of non-Hodgkin's lymphoma, a type of leukaemia.[27]

Bearing in mind the near-inevitable disagreement between the public, professionals and politicians, a better understanding of ethical issues is needed. It will allow decision-makers to realise what values underpin their decisions, where their judgements are inconsistent and where they are being unfair.

Rationing alternatives: theoretical concerns

The following sections will consider how ethical theory might inform the rationing debate. Firstly, cost-effectiveness and utilitarian views will be discussed. Secondly, concerns of equity, rights theory and Rawlsian interpretations of distributive justice will be outlined.

Cost-effectiveness and the utilitarian view

It is often said the NHS needs to be a cost-effective service. There are many examples of initiatives in promoting cost-effectiveness in the NHS at present, for example the use of Quality Adjusted Life Years and Marginal Analysis techniques.[28] The basic notion behind using cost-effectiveness criteria in rationing decisions is the concept of 'opportunity cost'; if health resources are used for one person they will not be available to others.[29] This implies that resources should be used in such a way that they achieve maximal *overall* benefit,[30] in terms of the population's *health*.[31]

Adequate decisions can be made using only cost-effectiveness criteria when two treatments, although leading to a similar outcome, vary greatly in cost.[32] An example is of two differently priced drugs, which have similar side effect profiles, but produce similar effects. It makes obvious sense to use the cheaper drug. Adequate decisions can also be made where the outcomes differ, but can be measured on a similar scale, as reduction in blood pressure can be, for example.

The cost and effectiveness of treatments are always relevant when health care must be prioritised. However, comparisons between treatments and costs are not easy. Firstly, it is not always clear how health benefits can be measured and compared.[33] Secondly, there are many treatments used regularly, which have yet to be fully evaluated for their cost-effectiveness.[34] Thirdly, some beneficial treatments may never demonstrate effectiveness.[35] For example, studies of treatments for the homeless are difficult to conduct, because of the high drop-out rates of these people from the studies.

As well as the practical difficulties in comparing costs and effectiveness of treatments, a question remains whether they are the only relevant criteria in making prioritisation decisions.

Utilitarianism theory

Using only cost-effectiveness criteria to allocate health care resources can be defended by utilitarian theory, if 'benefit' is equated with health gain for the population.

There are two main types of utilitarianism. In the simple or 'act' utilitarian view, the morality of an individual's actions must be judged only by the overall consequences of a particular action. The only action that is morally justified is that leading to the best overall consequences.[36] In health care, consequences are usually more narrowly interpreted as health outcome for patients rather than for the whole population.

This utilitarian approach necessitates a very complex analysis of the situation to enable one to decide what are the best overall consequences.[37] Strictly speaking, an 'act' utilitarian should calculate the harms and benefits (e.g. costs and outcomes) of giving or not giving treatment to a patient in every single case to ensure that maximal utility (health benefit) is attained. This would obviously lead to a highly inefficient state of affairs, where a great deal of time was spent on deciding whether or not to treat individual patients. In many cases it is not possible to make these accurate calculations, because of lack of information or evidence.

To overcome the standard objections to utilitarianism there is an alternative view, 'rule' utilitarianism, which avoids the need for such complicated moral calculations in every single case. In rule utilitarianism, it is said that certain moral guidelines or 'rules' are needed to produce the best consequences overall, so that resources are not wasted on individual calculations.[38] Such moral rules would be derived from existing knowledge of what produces the most benefit overall.

An example of 'rule' utilitarianism is seen in Quality Adjusted Life Years (QALYs: see below). QALYs can be weighted to account for social variables such as the number of dependants a patient has[39] or the 'need' for health care.[40] There is a logistic problem in using 'guiding rules' to decide priorities in health care under a utilitarian framework. Their use seems to be moving away from the basic point of utilitarianism, which is to maximise overall health gain in every individual case. In short, the rules seem too inflexible to produce *maximal* overall benefit. The tension between the need for overall and for individual benefit makes utilitarianism an unstable compromise, which indicates that other ethical frameworks are needed to resolve the dilemmas of health care resource allocation.[41] At the very least, some justification is needed for the weighting factors adopted.

An example of utilitarian thinking: Quality Adjusted Life Years

QALYs are the most frequently quoted example of utilitarian thinking in the NHS, as a validated measure of cost-effectiveness. The Quality Adjusted Life Year is a means of trying to quantify numerically the benefits and harms conferred on patients when they receive or fail to receive specific medical treatments. A numerical value is assigned to a year of life expectancy in a particular health state. The principle behind the system assumes that we can estimate the value to us of a year of life with a certain degree of distress or disability, as compared with the value to us of a year of healthy life. The cost of achieving that year of life expectancy is calculated giving the cost-per-QALY of a health care activity. It is comparable to the utilitarian approach in so far as it seeks to maximise the good consequences of a particular treatment.

Singer states that

> In essence, the QALY says that the value we get from spending money on healthcare can be measured in terms of the number of years of life gained, as long as we provide an appropriate rate of discount for periods in which, as a result of ill-health or disability, the quality of life is poorer. Several techniques have been used to establish the appropriate rate of discount. The most direct of these, the *time trade-off*, asks people how long a period of life in the given health condition they would be prepared to trade for one year of normal health. For example, they may say that for one year in normal health, they would give up two years bedridden. Then the appropriate rate of discount for being bedridden is 0.5, because that is the rate of quality adjustment at which a gain of two life-years when bedridden equals a gain of one year in normal health.[42]

QALYs are used in the context of decisions about rationing. The cost per QALY is calculated, and those activities that have the lowest cost per QALY (those that cost the least in relation to the improvement they make to the patient's life) are given priority. This decision-making process can be used to decide how money is spent between types of health care for the *population* or between different types of treatment for *one individual*.[43]

What are the problems in using QALYs?

There are several objections to the use of the QALY as a way of measuring the value gained by a given unit of health care expenditure. Most of these criticisms can be applied to all utilitarian approaches to health care resource allocation.

There has been much criticism of the research behind the development of QALY indices. The research has been seen to be inconsistent and invalid in that the numeric indices assigned to various quality of life states have varied with the different populations tested. For instance, doctors tend to assign lower numeric values to states of disability than the public.[44] In other words they are less happy than most people about the quality of life with disability. As well as this, there is often insufficient data to compare the effectiveness of rival treatments. For example, there may be no studies on the level of disability or quality of life for patients with a particular clinical condition before and after an intervention.

Others question whether it is possible, on a single index, to measure the complex features which contribute to a person's life in a meaningful way.[45] These features are seen to be non-comparable. As well as this, some others challenge the assumption that the numerical values of the quality of life measures truly reflect the values which people attach to their lives when in different health states.[46] That is, they doubt that one year of life of full quality really is equivalent to ten years of life at a tenth of that quality.

The unweighted QALY approach is said to lead to unjust social distribution, as it does not necessarily account for health care 'need' but only the 'capacity to benefit'.[47] For example, two populations with a similar prevalence of cancer may be competing for resources to fund a health promotion project to prevent cancer. One population has a high level of disability and one does not. The QALY approach would favour the relatively healthy population, since the potential to increase the quality of life is greater.

In this way the QALY approach may further disadvantage the vulnerable unless an adjustment is made in the QALY calculation to account for health care 'need'. An example of such an adjustment is found in 'equity weighted QALYs'.

Principle of equity

In view of the critique of using only cost-effectiveness criteria to decide health care priorities, it is important to consider other ethical principles or theories which may be used in resource allocation decisions, for example, the principle of equity.

This principle is now widely quoted as an important one to consider when making rationing decisions. However, there is considerable debate about what health services should be trying to equalise: is it access to health services, health outcomes or the amount spent on health care? Furthermore, there is confusion about what is meant by equity and equality.[48] For example, in the amount spent on health care, the distinction is made as follows. Rationing health care with 'equality' means that resources are allotted in equal shares regardless of 'need' and is essentially a description; the term 'equity', however, refers to a distribution of resources that is linked to some concept of health care need[49] and hence has a normative element. So the term 'equity' requires a fuller definition.[50]

In the context of rationing health care in the NHS, we might interpret the principle of equity as implying a duty to provide health care access (at least to a minimal or reasonable standard) for all. An alternative interpretation would be a duty to reduce health inequality between different social groups. These considerations are similar to those expressed by some rights theorists and by those advocating a Rawlsian approach to health care resource allocation.

Rights theory: relation to the 'decent minimum'

Rights theory can be seen to support the principle of promoting equity in health service provision, if all individuals are seen to have a right to access a high level of health care. This section will outline how rights can be defined and derived from a community consensus on morality and applied to define a basic core or 'decent minimum' of services available to all.

What are moral rights?

Most people can easily understand the notion of legal rights, but moral rights are more difficult to appreciate and define.[51] Moral rights are often appealed to as eternal and universal truths (the rights have always existed and belong to everyone), although their source is often felt to be obscure. Many people claim that they have 'rights to health care' but it is not clear what this really means in practice.

John Stuart Mill suggested that rights have corresponding *duties* (or responsibilities).[52] Rights can be thought of as justified claims or entitlements that can be validated by moral principles or rules. This can be understood further by considering that rights can be classified into: *positive or claim rights* which demand action from others, or *negative* rights, which require that the person be allowed to act in a certain way without being restricted by others. A right to health care usually implies a positive right, where the health service has a duty to provide a particular service.

Where two groups of patients require health care, but there is only enough money to treat one group, there is a problem deciding what action would be morally justified. If two patients have a right to health care in the way described, a person responsible for funding is obliged to act to respect all rights and give both patients treatment, which is clearly impossible.

Hart offers another useful definition of a right: 'The concept of a right belongs to that branch of morality which is specifically concerned to determine when the person's freedom may be limited by another's'.[53] This is a useful definition in that it allows us to see that whether a patient has a right to a particular treatment can depend on the context of the case. In the context of resource allocation, patients may claim that they have a right to a particular type of health care. However, their freedom to claim treatment is limited by the resources which are needed to treat others.

In this view, rights are not necessarily absolute and often, in the case of conflicting rights, one right may be considered overriding.[54] Rights which are not absolute are referred to as prima facie rights. If rights are not absolute, but prima facie, they may be better understood as contextual phenomena, which do not possess the qualities of universality and eternality. If two patients could benefit from a treatment, but there are only enough resources to treat one, then whether each patient has a 'right' to treatment will depend on many factors. Such factors might include the cost, the effectiveness of the treatment and the patient's clinical condition. For example, a person in the UK may have a 'right' to a reasonable standard of health care. However, the definition of what is reasonable is influenced by what is customary practice in the UK for other health care users.

How can rights be justified?

Rights are sometimes considered to promote selfish action as they are seen as the concerns of individuals. However, rights can also *protect* individuals from exploitation by defining the limits of acceptable behaviour and entitlement in a community, for example the level of health care to which everyone is entitled.

Rights can be grounded in terms of a presumed consensus on morality within a *community*. This communitarian notion of a right implies that the community has some common moral ground. From this common moral ground, the community can agree that in certain circumstances some actions should be compulsory or some should be outlawed. These considerations give rise to the possible claims and duties which are the basis of rights for each individual.[55] The right to effective treatment when one is seriously ill might be particularly clear as this has been defined as a health care priority by the public in several public surveys. But there is a danger in seeing rights simply as something communally agreed. For instance, some communities may not agree on 'rights' such as basic health care, and deny it to some of their citizens.

However, in the context of priority setting we might assume that a general right to *basic health care* provision will benefit the whole of society and could be morally justified. Although health care users do not necessarily have a right to claim health care in *all* circumstances, it seems reasonable to suggest that they all have a right to access health care in our society in most circumstances. If they are suffering from a condition for which an effective remedy is available, then treatment should be provided unless certain other criteria apply. For example, the treatment is particularly expensive or there is a cheaper alternative or the probability of benefit is small.

The summation of effective, but inexpensive, services could be thought to constitute a *basic core* or *decent minimum* of services to which every individual is entitled. If this definition of core services were to allow a *high* level of access to health care, then this approach may achieve the same aims as promoting equitable access.

What are the problems in using rights theory?

Appeals to rights are seen to encourage conflict and selfish behaviour and to ignore actions which would promote the good of the community. For example, it might be decided that one patient had the right to an organ transplant but two other people would be denied health care as a result.[56]

If 'a right to health care' involves a low level of access to health services, then inequity may result if, for instance, some members of the public purchase medical services privately. Such inequity is seen in the USA, which has a health care framework based on minimal entitlements.[57]

Rights theory cannot tell us whether or not the Health Service should fund debatable or marginal treatments, which are not included in a 'basic core', such as coronary artery bypass grafting for smokers and reversal of sterilisation operations.

These criticisms are not to suggest that rights are inherently adversarial or that they are dispensable, but rather to note that rights theory is only a *partial* framework in informing the rationing debate.[58] Ethical theories need not be used in isolation. It might be possible to adopt a 'compound approach' to health care rationing, where a basic set of health services are defined by rights theory and a utilitarian framework is used to decide how resources should be spent on more expensive treatments.

Rawlsian theory

Another approach which supports the principle of promoting equity in the health services is that offered by Rawls. In this model, equity of *outcome* as well as *access* to health care is considered. He suggests that, generally, one should approach distributive justice by considering that it is a co-operative venture. Rawls assumes that only through co-operation will we all benefit maximally. Hence, health care resource decisions need to be made by consensus. He suggests that we should imagine what decision-makers would decide if beforehand they could ignore their own social circumstances, for example, their level of wealth, health status, etc. Rawls considers the differences in health or wealth between persons to be generally undeserved and a distraction to the process of fair decision-making. So decisions about the distribution of health care, as about other goods, should be made behind a 'veil of ignorance' about what the status of the decision-makers will be within the society.

There are two overriding moral principles to consider in this model of distributive justice. First, 'each person has an equal right to the most extensive liberty compatible with a like liberty for all'. Namely, in the context of health, every person has a right at least to *access* a reasonably high level of health care, so that they might flourish as a human being. Second, inequality in the distribution should only be tolerated if it results in benefit for every member of society.[59] For example, in the context of health care a few patients might receive very expensive cardiac pacemakers instead of cheaper ones, to allow medical science to develop and benefit everyone in the long term.

The process of Rawlsian decision-making is as follows. Firstly, 'considered judgements' are collected. Considered judgements are defined by Rawls as moral statements which are 'most likely to be displayed without distortion'. An example of a 'considered judgement' might be that health care workers should not exploit patients for their own gain. The considered judgements and the moral requirements to promote equality and liberty are then synthesised into morally validated principles, that is, statements applicable to a wide variety of decisions in health care resource allocation.

The principles might give general guidance about what type of care or what group of patients should be given priority for health care, for instance the seriously ill or the socially disadvantaged. These principles are not absolute, but are subject to constant pruning and revision as incoherent results emerge. This is called the process of 'reflective equilibrium'.[60]

What are the problems in using Rawlsian theory?

The major problem with the process of Rawlsian decision-making is that it is not immediately clear how to apply it to the dilemmas of health care resource allocation when resources are scarce. Even if one were able to define the considered judgements that were relevant to the process, it is not obvious how to balance the requirements for equality and liberty so that one is able to create morally validated principles which could be applied to many health care purchasing dilemmas. The principles promoting 'liberty' and 'equality' do not clarify whether the elimination of differences in health status between *social groups* or *individuals* is a priority. For example, it is unclear whether services in effective health promotion for the socially disadvantaged would receive precedence over services to treat the seriously ill.

However, it is still possible to consider the 'spirit' of the Rawlsian concept of resource allocation and realise that such a theory might lead us to different purchasing conclusions from those reached by utilitarian theory. In Rawlsian theory there is a much greater emphasis on addressing health inequality and on a presumed 'social contract'. Arguably, this paradigm might result in an even more equitable distribution of health care resources than the rights theory model, since any inequalities in service provision would have to be shown to benefit society as a whole or they would not be tolerated.

Does it matter which ethical framework is used?

It is obvious that there will be occasions when we can reach rationing decisions on health care which satisfy the principle of equity/ rights-based/Rawlsian theory and the need for cost-effectiveness/ utilitarian theory. For example, the implementation of a vaccination programme for childhood diseases in a deprived inner-city area would be preferred to the development of a new technology dietetic assessment unit in a local hospital.

However, the pursuit of policies to minimise inequity is often inconsistent with a policy of cost-effectiveness.[61] Cost-effectiveness tends to imply that policies should lead to maximal or aggregate benefit per unit cost. Such policies tend to promote the health of the majority. However, the pursuit of policies which respect the principle of equity and humanity are often orientated towards improving the health of vulnerable and disadvantaged groups, so they at least achieve a minimal or reasonable standard of health.[62]

A health district may need to decide whether to spend its health promotion money on a coronary heart disease prevention programme for the general public or on AIDS education for local prostitutes. Both programmes are known to work in practice, but the coronary heart disease prevention programme is more cost-effective. The concerns of cost-effectiveness will therefore favour the former programme, the principle of equity – relating to need – the latter. In terms of ethical theories, it seems likely that a Rawlsian interpretation would fund the AIDS education programme as the prostitutes are already a disadvantaged group. In contrast to this, utilitarian theory would advise the coronary heart disease programme, as it is more cost-effective. It does not seem that rights-based theory can help us resolve this dilemma. It would be difficult to argue that either group had a right to a specialist health promotion project which was not open to everyone in society.

Conclusion

In conclusion, there seems to be a general trend to more explicit health care rationing in the UK. Those making rationing policies need to consider ethical issues before decisions are made. The consideration of ethical theory allows the values behind decision-making to become clearer and the choice of ethical framework used can have a profound effect on how resources are distributed. Also, policy decision-makers are able to realise where their judgements are inconsistent and where they are being unfair.

There are however, limitations in the use of ethical theory in the context of health care resource allocation. The theories are not pre-scriptive of which treatments should or should not be funded in every case and there may be disagreement by policy-makers over which theory to adopt and how it is implemented. Some of these difficulties can be overcome by using a 'compound approach', where theoretical frameworks are used in combination.

Notes

1 Harrison, S. and Hunter, D. J. (1994) *Rationing Healthcare*, Institute for Public Policy Research, pp. 14–22.
2 Weale, A. (1995) 'The Ethics of Rationing', *British Medical Bulletin*, vol. 51, no. 4, p. 831.
3 Ham, C. (1992) *Health Policy in Britain: The Politics and Organisation of the National Health Service*, Macmillan, p. 245. Ham, C. and Appleby, J. (1993) *The Future Direction of the NHS*, National Association of Health Authorities and Trusts, p. 1.
4 Ham (1992) *Health Policy in Britain*, p. 41.
5 Weale (1995) 'The Ethics of Rationing', p. 833. Gray, M. J. A. (1979) 'Choosing Priorities', *Journal of Medical Ethics*, vol. 5, pp. 73–4.
6 Ham and Appleby, *Future Direction of the NHS*, p. 1.
7 Calman, K. C. (1994) 'The Ethics of Allocation of Scarce Healthcare Resources: A View From the Centre', *Journal of Medical Ethics*, vol. 20, p. 74. Heginbotham, C. (1992) 'The Future of Healthcare', *British Medical Journal*, vol. 18, pp. 33–6. Ham (1992) *Health Policy in Britain*, p. 60.
8 Hancock, C. (1994) 'Getting a Quart out a of a Pint Pot, Rationing in Action', *British Medical Journal*, vol. 18, pp. 17–18. Ham (1992) *Health Policy in Britain*, p. 40.

9 Lockwood, M. (1988) 'Quality of Life and Resource Allocation', in J. M. Bell and S. Mendus (eds) *Philosophy and Medical Welfare*, Oxford University Press, pp. 33–4. Ham and Appleby (1993) *Future Direction of the NHS*, pp. 5–8.

10 Ham (1992) *Health Policy in Britain*, p. 63.

11 Underwood, M. J. and Bailey, J. S. (1993) 'Should Smokers Be Offered Coronary By-Pass Surgery?', *British Medical Journal*, vol. 306, pp. 1047–8. Shaw, A. B. (1994) 'In Defence of Ageism', *Journal of Medical Ethics*, vol. 20, pp. 189–90.

12 Klein, R. and Redmayne, S. (1992) *Patterns of Priorities: A Study of the Purchasing and Rationing Policies of Health Authorities*, National Association of Health Authorities and Trusts, Research Paper No. 7, p. 892. Ham (1992) *Health Policy in Britain*, p. 63.

13 Ham (1992) *Health Policy in Britain*, pp. 17–30. Seedhouse, D. (1994) *Fortress NHS: A Philosophical Review of the National Health Service*, John Wiley & Sons, pp. 15–17. Maxwell, R. J. (1996) 'The R-Word', *The Newsletter of the King's Fund*, vol. 19 (summer), p. 1. Maxwell, R. J. (1995) 'Why Rationing is on the Agenda', *British Medical Bulletin*, vol. 51, no. 4, p. 761. Harrison and Hunter (1994) *Rationing Healthcare*, pp. 32–8.

14 Harris, T. (1994) 'Consulting the Public, Rationing in Action', *British Medical Journal*, vol. 18, pp. 160–1.

15 Honigsbaum, F., Richards, J. and Lockett, T. (1995) *Priority Setting in Action: Purchasing Dilemmas*, Radcliffe Medical Press, p. 10. Ham, C. (1996) *The New NHS: A Guide For Board Members*, National Association of Health Authorities and Trusts, p. 3.

16 Seedhouse (1994) *Fortress NHS*, p. 27.

17 Price, D. (1996) 'Lessons for Healthcare Rationing from the Case of Child B', *British Medical Journal*, vol. 312 (20 Jan.), p. 167.

18 Walley, T. and Barton, S. (1995) 'A Purchaser Perspective of Managing New Drugs: Interferon Beta as a Case Study', *British Medical Journal*, vol. 311 (23 Sept.), p. 796. Maxwell (1996) 'The R-Word', p. 2.

19 Klein, R., Day, P. and Redmayne, S. (1995) 'Rationing in the NHS: The Dance of the Seven Veils – in Reverse', *British Medical Bulletin*, vol. 51, no. 4, p. 773.

20 New, B. (1996) 'The Rationing Agenda in the NHS', *British Medical Journal*, vol. 312, pp. 1593–601. Honigsbaum et al. (1995) *Priority Setting in Action*, pp. 11–12. Maxwell (1996) 'The R-Word', p. 1. Klein et al. (1995) 'Rationing in the NHS', p. 770.

21 Delamothe, T. (1991) 'Social Inequalities in Health', *British Medical Journal*, vol. 303 (26 Oct.), p. 1047. Acheson, D. (1995) 'Summary', in M. Benzeval, K. Judge and M. Whitehead (eds) *Tackling Inequalities in Health: An Agenda for Action*, King's Fund, p. xviii. Ham and Appleby (1993) *Future Direction of the NHS*, p. 4. Beck, E. J. and Adam, S. A. (eds) (1990) *The White Paper and Beyond*, Oxford Medical Publications, pp. 4–5. Scambler, G. (1991) *Sociology as Applied to Medicine*, Balliere and Tindall, pp. 109–28. Acheson, D. (1998) *Independent Enquiry into Inequalities in Health*, Report, HMSO.

22 New (1996) 'The Rationing Agenda in the NHS', pp. 1594–9.

23 Ham, C. (1995) 'Synthesis: What Can We Learn From International Experience', *British Medical Bulletin*, vol. 51, no. 4, pp. 819–30.

24 Redmayne, S. (1996) *Small Steps Big Goals: Purchasing Policies in the NHS*, National Association of Health Authorities and Trusts, Research Paper No. 21, p. 7, pp. 1591–3. Lenaghan, J., New, B. and Mitchell, M. (1996) 'Setting Priorities: Is there a Role for Citizens' Juries?', *British Medical Journal*, vol. 312, pp. 1591–3.

25 Klein, R. (1994) 'Dimensions of Rationing: Who Should Do What?, Rationing in Action', *British Medical Journal*, vol. 18, pp. 100–4.

26 Redmayne (1996) *Small Steps Big Goals*, p. 15. New (1996) 'The Rationing Agenda', p. 1597.

27 Dixon, J. and Welch, G. H. (1991) 'Priority Setting: Lessons from Oregon', *The Lancet*, vol. 337 (13 April), pp. 891–2. Daniels, N. (1993) 'Is the Oregon Rationing Plan Fair?', in T. L. Beauchamp and L. Walters (eds) *Contemporary Issues in Bioethics*, International Thomson Publishing, pp. 742–5.

28 Honigsbaum *et al.* (1995) *Priority Setting in Action*, pp. 74–9. Drummond, M. F. (1985) *Principles of Economic Appraisal in Healthcare*, Oxford Medical Publications, pp. 20–2.

29 Robinson (1993) 'Economic Evaluation and Healthcare', *British Medical Journal*, vol. 307, p. 924. Seedhouse (1994) *Fortress NHS*, pp. 82–3. Mooney, G., Gerard, K., Donaldson, C. and Ferrar, S. (1992) *Priority Setting in Purchasing: Some Practical Guidelines*, National Association of Health Authorities and Trusts, Research Paper No. 6, p. 7.

30 Robinson (1993) 'Economic Evaluation', p. 671. Mooney, G. H. (1986) *Economics, Medicine and Healthcare*, Wheatsheaf Books, pp. 7–8, 15. Donaldson, C. (1994) 'Economics of Priority Setting: Let's Ration Rationally!, Rationing in Action', *British Medical Journal*, vol. 18, p. 81. Jones, C. (1993) 'Purchasing Cost-effective Social Care', in M. F. Drummond and A. Maynard (eds) *Purchasing and Providing Cost-effective Healthcare*, Churchill Livingstone, p. 178.

31 Weale (1995) 'Ethics of Rationing', p. 831. Ham (1992) *Health Policy in Britain*, pp. 53–3. Ham and Appleby (1993) *Future Direction of the NHS*, pp. 3–4.

32 Robinson (1993) 'Economic Evaluation', pp. 726–7. Seedhouse (1994) *Fortress NHS*, pp. 82–3.

33 Chadwick, R. (1994) 'Justice in Priority Setting, Rationing in Action', *British Medical Journal*, vol. 18, p. 83.

34 Hoare, J. (1992) *Tidal Wave: New Technology, Medicine and the NHS*, King's Fund, pp. 8–14.

35 Calman, K. C. (1994) 'Ethics of Allocation', p. 72.

36 Williams, B. (1991) *Morality: An Introduction to Ethics*, Cambridge University Press, pp. 96–7. Beauchamp, T. L. and Childress, J. (1994) *Principles of Biomedical Ethics*, Oxford University Press, pp. 47–50.

37 Williams, B. (1991) *Morality*, pp. 100–5.

38 Ibid., pp. 105–7. Griffin, J. (1982) 'Modern Utilitarianism', in *Revue Internationale de Philosophie*, vol. 36, pp. 350–3.

39 Williams, A. (1996) 'Economics of Coronary Artery Bypass Grafting', *British Medical Journal*, vol. 291 (326), p. 327.

40 Nord, E. (1996) 'Health Status Index Models for Use in Resource Allocation Decisions: A Critical Review in the Light of Observed Preferences for Social Choice', *International Journal of Technology Assessment in Health Care*, vol. 12, no. 1, pp. 31–44.
41 Williams (1991) *Morality*, pp. 107–8. Nord (1996) 'Health Status Index Models', pp. 31–44.
42 Singer, A., McKie, J., Kuhse, H. and Richardson, J. (1995) 'Double Jeopardy and the Use of QALYs in Health Care Allocation', *Journal of Medical Ethics*, vol. 21, pp. 144–50.
43 Williams, A. (1996) 'Economics of Coronary Artery Bypass Grafting', pp. 326–9.
44 Ibid., p. 327.
45 Lockwood, M. (1988) 'Quality of Life and Resource Allocation', in J. M. Bell and S. Mendus (eds) *Philosophy and Medical Welfare*, Oxford University Press, pp. 35–6.
46 Ibid., p. 40.
47 Beauchamp and Childress (1994) *Principles of Biomedical Ethics*, pp. 54–5.
48 Mooney *et al.* (1992) *Priority Setting in Purchasing*, p. 9. President's Commission for the Study of Ethical Problems in Medicine and Biomedical and Behavioural Research (1993) in T. L. Beauchamp and L. Walters (eds) *Contemporary Issues in Bioethics*, International Thomson Publishing, pp. 684–5.
49 Jones (1993) 'Purchasing Cost-effective Social Care', p. 179.
50 Harrison and Hunter (1994) *Rationing Healthcare*, p. 54.
51 Beauchamp and Childress (1994) *Principles of Biomedical Ethics*, p. 76.
52 Mill, J. S. (1972) 'On Moral Obligation and Justice', ch. 5 in *Utilitarianism*, ed. H. B. Acton, J. M. Dent and Sons, pp. 40–2.
53 Hart, H. L. A. (1984) 'Are There Any Natural Rights?, in J. Waldon (ed.) *Theories of Rights*, Oxford University Press, p. 79.
54 Beauchamp and Childress (1994) *Principles of Biomedical Ethics*, p. 72.
55 Ibid., pp. 71–2.
56 Ibid., pp. 76–7.
57 Light, D. (1994) 'Managed Care: False and Real Solutions', *The Lancet*, vol. 344, pp. 1197–9.
58 Beauchamp and Childress (1994) *Principles of Biomedical Ethics*, 76–7.
59 Rawls, J. (1990) 'Justice as Fairness' and a theory of justice' (1971), in R. C. Solomon and H. Murphy (eds) *What is Justice?*, Oxford University Press, pp. 306–7.
60 Beauchamp and Childress (1994) *Principles of Biomedical Ethics*, pp. 20–1.
61 Bradshaw, G. and Bradshaw, P. L. (1995) 'The Equity Debate within the British National Health Service', *Journal of Nursing Management*, vol. 3, pp. 161–8.
62 Chadwick (1994) 'Justice in Priority Setting', pp. 92–5. Donaldson (1994) 'Economics of Priority Setting', p. 81.

2

ETHICS AND THE EXTRA-CONTRACTUAL REFERRAL: A CASE STUDY FROM NORTHAMPTONSHIRE HEALTH AUTHORITY

Henrietta Ewart

Introduction

The extra-contractual referral (ECR) was an administrative and financial device whereby doctors could refer and health authorities could fund patients to be treated at institutions other than those providing the majority of care for a given authority. The need for this device resulted from the creation of the NHS 'internal market' in the Conservative Government White Paper, *Working for Patients*, published in 1989.

Under the subsequent legislation, health authorities were required to enter into service agreements with those institutions providing the majority of care for local residents. The ECR provided a device for 'one off' care of individuals outside these arrangements.

The Labour Government published a White Paper in 1998, *The New NHS*, which will dismantle many of the structures of the internal market. One of the changes ends the current arrangements for ECRs from 31 March 1999. Primary Care Groups, bringing together the general practitioners responsible for care in localities of, on average, about 100,000 people, will be responsible for many of the decisions about where patients receive care. However, the resources available to them will still be limited and the need to make difficult decisions about resource allocation will remain. The lessons learnt from developing policy on ECRs will still be highly relevant within the new framework.

General concerns

Under the 1998 arrangements for the National Health Service in England and Wales, health authorities receive a fixed budget with which to purchase all the health care required by their residents. This budget is calculated to a formula designed to reflect the size of the population and its health needs, as indicated by the age and sex structure and socio-economic characteristics of that population. Since the National Health Service and Community Care Act of 1990,[1] the majority of health care purchasing is achieved by the health authority developing service agreements with a variety of hospitals or other institutions for an agreed level of activity (e.g. out-patient visits, procedures, day case-work, investigations, etc.) at an agreed cost. This enables the authorities, and the hospitals with which they contract, to manage their budgets. It also enables the health authorities to ensure that a balanced portfolio of care is available to cover the majority of their residents' health care needs, both emergency and planned.

Under this system, however, there is always the possibility that a number of people will seek referral to an institution with which their health authority does not hold an agreement. The administrative device by which this can be accomplished is known as an extra-contractual referral (ECR) and is a method of cost-per-case charging.

It was a much vaunted intention of the 1989 Government White Paper *Working for Patients* to 'make the money follow the patient'.[2] This was intended to mean that health care institutions would be remunerated in accordance with the number of patients treated. However, it was interpreted by many doctors, and also patients, to mean that they should have complete freedom of referral and that funding should be arranged accordingly.

In practice, although in aggregate it is possible to 'make the money follow the patient' (i.e. to set agreements with the institutions that would treat the majority of local patients), this does not work so well in the case of individual patients wishing to seek treatment outside of such agreements. The health authority's resources are insufficient to allow unrestricted access to ECRs, not least because the costs of ECRs are, on average, at least twice the cost of similar care within an agreement.[3] In addition, there is no mechanism for moving funds out of an existing agreement to pay for similar care elsewhere.

The reasons why patients or their doctors might seek referral via the ECR mechanism are many and varied. However, the majority of ECRs are sought for care that could have been provided within service agreements.[4] For example: the patient has moved into an authority area from elsewhere and wishes to continue the care that began at a distant hospital; the patient has been recommended a particular hospital or consultant (often through a patient support group); the patient wishes to be treated close to other family members.

Another important group of ECR requests arise when patients require treatment that cannot be provided under an agreement. This might include highly specialised treatment for a very rare disorder that might only be needed once in a year, or less frequently, by a particular authority. This level of activity could not be covered efficiently by a service agreement. Sometimes a patient wishes to have access to a very new, experimental and possibly incompletely evaluated treatment which may only be available at one centre.

In addition to these situations, most health authorities have a list of procedures or treatments that they do not normally purchase.[5] These lists have been developed in the face of severe resource constraints in order to divert resources from care considered as 'low priority' and conserve them for higher-priority services. Most health authorities do not routinely purchase cosmetic treatments (e.g. nose reshaping, breast enlargement, liposuction for obesity, removal of tatoos, etc.) and may also exclude other procedures such as sterilisation or in-vitro fertilisation. Funding can, though, be considered for individual cases where such a procedure can be shown to be a priority; they would then be funded via an ECR.

It can be seen that this system has the potential to create a tension between patients (and their doctors) and the funding authorities. If the patient's right to choose and the doctor's right to refer wherever they choose is always respected this will quickly become unsustainable by existing resources. Allowing some patients and doctors complete freedom of choice in this way will quickly limit the choice available to others (since there will be less money available to them). Health authorities therefore require a means of legitimately restricting this freedom of choice in order to conserve resources for the benefit of all residents.

A further reason for restricting the flow of resources into ECRs is the need to protect resources for planned investment with, mainly local, providers of health care via service agreements. Purchasing the majority of care through such agreements has allowed us to build a portfolio of high quality, accessible and affordable services to meet most health care needs. It also enables relationships to be formed between the authority and clinicians or Trusts which shape a longer-term view of how services will need to develop in response to changing need or changes in medical practice. This is in contrast to ECRs which are, essentially, 'one off' random flows of individuals to a wide range of different providers. If ECR flows become large enough, there is a risk that they will destabilise the authority's strategic plans for local services, by drawing money and activity away from them.

A local solution

Northamptonshire Health Authority responded to this challenge by developing and widely publishing a policy on elective ECRs. This was developed by a multi-disciplinary group including representation from the health authority, local consultants, general practitioners and the Community Health Councils. The work started by agreeing which concerns should underlie decisions on individual ECRs. These included:

Concern that decisions should be equitable. ECRs should not enable an individual to gain advantage in terms of care otherwise denied to the rest of the population, such as a reduction in waiting time.

Concern that decisions should be consistent with health authority strategy. ECRs should be in line with the agreed strategic aims of the Health Authority.

Concern to ensure that treatments are not harmful and will be of benefit to patients. Clear evidence for effectiveness will be expected for treatments to be funded as ECRs.

In addition, some principles based on good clinical practice were also developed, examples of these are:

> We believe it is in the patients' own best interests for them to be known to and managed by local services in the majority of cases. This improves convenience and access for the patient – in line with the wishes of the majority of patients. In addition, it means that the case is familiar to the local hospital which will aid future management, particularly should emergency care be required.

Patients with a chronic or progressive disorder should almost always be under the care of local services. Such patients receiving care at distant centres (i.e. as ECRs) tend to become lost to local services and may end up in a position where no one clinician is managing their overall care. This is likely to be detrimental to the patient's management.

These principles were applied to the situations that commonly give rise to requests for ECRs in order to create a framework for decision-making. When applied to individual patient cases, they give very little weight to the individual's (or the referring doctor's) right to choose. Unfortunately, where resources are limited this is always likely to be the case, since the health authority has to balance the potential benefit to the individual of free choice against the opportunities lost as a result of committing resources in this way. Nevertheless, only rarely is treatment denied. More usually patients are asked to seek similar care at a provider with which there is an agreement.

However, in order to ensure that the individual's perspective received consideration and in order to make the decision process more explicit, we developed an 'Ethical framework to decide on ECR funding' (Figure 2.1). This was done by asking the multi-disciplinary group to consider a series of hypothetical cases. For each case, the principles behind the group's decisions were identified and discussed. The relative importance of the different principles was also considered. The result was a flow chart outlining the decision process.

The policy developed by the multidisciplinary group was then further developed through discussion with existing advisory groups (including the Local Medical Committee of general practitioners and the GP Commissioning Group, which was a forum through which GPs gave commissioning advice to the health authority). The final policy was adopted through the formal mechanism of a health authority meeting that was open to the public.

The policy is implemented through three levels. First, doctors should bear the policy guidance in mind before considering a referral which may result in an ECR. Second, if there clearly are good reasons for an ECR, in line with the policy, the funding can be agreed through liaison with the Public Health Department of the health authority. Finally, if the case is complex or an acceptable

it is not feasible to develop a local service under a service agreement. The health authority therefore approves funding.

The hospital in London recommends a particular type of chemotherapy. The health authority explores the possibility of providing this locally, both to save costs and reduce travelling for the patient. This is not possible because the local specialists have no experience of the treatment. Therefore, the health authority approves funding for the care to be given at the hospital in London. The health authority also recommends the continuing involvement of local services so that local care (palliative care, specialist nursing services, etc.) can be organised if required.

In making this decision, we have attempted to achieve the best outcome for the patient. Because very few Northamptonshire residents will develop mesothelioma, we feel it is justified to use ECR funding to obtain highly specialised care on the few occasions it will be required.

Case 3

A couple seek advice for infertility from a consultant working in a private clinic in Northamptonshire. He suggests that their problem may be 'immunological' and refers them to an NHS clinic in London offering 'immunotherapy'. The treatment involves injecting white blood cells from the man into the woman. It would require ECR funding.

The health authority has concerns about the effectiveness of this treatment. We study the research literature and take the advice of specialist immunologists. Our opinion is that this treatment is of absolutely no proven benefit and carries measurable risks (viral transmission, etc.). We therefore refuse funding.

In making this decision, we have overridden the couple's right to make their own decision (since they wished to try any treatment that gave them hope of a pregnancy), because of the lack of evidence for effectiveness of the treatment, the potential risks of the treatment and the existing resource constraints.

Notes

1 National Health Service and Community Care Act, 1990, London: HMSO, 1990.
2 Working for Patients, Government White Paper, London: HMSO, 1989.

27

3 Personal communication, Northamptonshire Health Authority, Finance Directorate, 1997.
4 Northamptonshire Health Authority, Public Health and Finance Directorates, 1997.
5 Bill New, *The Rationing Agenda in the NHS*, London: King's Fund, 1996. Frank Honigsbaum, John Richards and Tony Locket, *Priority Setting in Action*, Oxford: Radcliffe Medical Press, 1995.

3

THE PRIORITISATION OF HEALTH CARE IN OXFORDSHIRE

Siân Griffiths

There is more demand for health care services than can be met from the budget allocated to Oxfordshire Health Authority (HA). In the absence of a national framework for priority-setting and as it was faced with difficult decisions and the need to refuse some treatments, Oxfordshire HA developed a Priorities Forum. The work of the Forum is underpinned by an ethical framework based on the criteria of *effectiveness, equity* and *patient choice*.

This chapter describes the evolution of the Forum, how the ethical framework has been used in practical situations, and some of the challenges from current changes of policy at a national level.

Background

Oxfordshire HA is responsible for the health of the population of the county. Set in central England, it has a population around 600,000 and is more rural than most areas in England and Wales. There are some small densely populated areas but the general nature of the county is of market towns and small villages. The relative affluence of the county means that its allocation of national resources for both health and social care is lower than average. The budget of the HA has historically tended to be in deficit. Financial pressures are compounded by the complexity of the health care system resulting from the interaction between Oxford University and the NHS. Whilst this relationship can be expensive, it is also an environment of exciting innovation – often as a result of the research in which local clinicians are involved. Managerial pressures to reduce costs,

29

combined with the clinical drive for new treatments and greater public expectations, create a situation in which difficult choices need to be made. These choices are made in a variety of ways: by individual clinicians deciding which treatments should or should not be initiated, by managers as they set budgets and agree spending plans, by commissioners as they agree contracts with service providers, and by regions or governments as they set priorities.

In the absence of a national system for priority-setting, local systems evolve. In Oxfordshire it was requests to the HA to pay for individual treatments, outside those planned in advance, that highlighted the need for an explicit, consistent and fair approach to decisions and led to the creation of the Priorities Forum.

Developing an approach to prioritisation

Reform of the NHS in the early 1990s introduced an 'internal market' with financial contracts between those purchasing services and those providing them. Contracts for services need to be agreed well in advance to allow stability and planning. Inevitably there are unforeseen requests for services outside these contracts. These needed to be paid for, and extra-contractual referrals (ECRs) were developed as the mechanism by which providers were reimbursed.

The 1995 finance director's report to the HA Board reported that the ECR budget was out of control, following an exponential rise in demand. It became apparent from board meetings that we had little understanding of the ECR process.

There were three main categories of ECRs: emergency, tertiary and elective. For emergency ECRs, there was no debate, these had to be paid for. If a resident of Oxfordshire fell while climbing in the Lake District or had appendicitis in Devon, then not only was there no administrative way of refusing to fund treatment, there was also no ethical justification for doing so. Tertiary ECRs were referrals made by one consultant to another for tertiary treatments outside contracts. These were not a major problem because, within Oxfordshire, most tertiary care was covered by existing contracts at the teaching hospitals and tertiary centres providing specialist services.

However, requests for new treatments were a subject for debate. Elective ECRs were the category of ECR for which the HA had most say, that is, where a there was a request for treatment outside existing contracts. In the early days these were agreed or refused using technical guidance. There was an informal system of obtaining clinical advice from the public health physicians. This advice depended on from whom it was sought. What was lacking was a consistent framework for making decisions, and an openness that these decisions were being made.

As a consequence of board discussions about ECRs, a group – which evolved into the Priorities Forum – started to meet to monitor the ECR process and to report back to the board. Initial meetings focused on individual cases and monitoring the spend on ECRs. It became obvious that a better understanding of the values used to make decisions was needed if we were to be able to make fair and consistent decisions and justify them. A small group, including a clinical ethicist and university lecturer in philosophy, met to develop an ethical framework. This was subsequently adopted by the HA.

It became obvious that the initial focus on choices about individuals was often at the margins and had little overall impact on the health care system. Members of the Forum felt it was important to tackle areas of mainstream clinical work, and discussions about issues such as thresholds for referral for renal replacement therapy were introduced. In addition, the difficulty of choosing between service areas was recognised as one which needed to be addressed. Other issues included devising a systematic way of discussing innovations in clinical practice, particularly new drugs, and of responding to guidance from the various bodies involved in systematic reviews, effectiveness assessment and guideline production. The development of a forum to address these issues is described in the rest of the chapter.

Establishing the priorities forum

The Priorities Forum is now a subcommittee of the HA, and formally reports its discussions and decisions to the public via board meetings. The history of the Priorities Forum is summarised in Table 3.1.

Meeting on a monthly basis, the Priorities Forum considers a rolling programme of issues on which discussion and decisions are needed. The current membership includes GPs, hospital doctors, managers, executive and non-executive members of the HA, and members of Oxford University Medical School. The Community Health Council (CHC), a body which represents the views of users

Table 3.1 History of the Priorities Forum

Nov. 94	ECR panel formed to monitor and control elective ECRs. Early membership has representation from GPs, Trusts, HA.
Feb. 95	ECR panel changes to Priorities Forum and starts to use individual cases to produce a body of case law and establish precedents on which to base future decisions.
Oct. 95	Expanded membership to include Medical Directors of Trusts, GPs involved in contracting, CHC with observer status.
Dec. 95	Drawing up of low priority list for surgical procedures.
Jan. 96	First discussion of introduction of new drugs.

Feb. 96	Meetings divided into two parts:
	   development of policy advice
	   consideration of ECRs.

Mar. 96	Clinicians starting to attend to talk about clinical management within the budgetary envelope of their specialties.
May 96	First set of lavender (policy) statements distributed to GPs and Trusts.
June 96	Formation of ethics subgroup to develop framework of principles.
Oct. 96	Seminar for HA on prioritisation.
April 97	District-wide seminar to launch ethical framework.
Sept. 97	Report to board with recommendations.
May 98	Seminar for the county, including primary care groups and local authorities.
July 98	Appeals process agreed.
Oct. 98	Public involvement programme initiated.

of the health services, regularly attends in observer capacity. Non-executives of the HA provide additional lay perspectives. Whether the CHC should have full membership has been discussed but the consensus is that the CHC should retain its ability to advocate for members of the public should they contest the Forum's decisions. Essential support is provided by the Reader in the University Deptartment of Public Health and Primary Care, who is trained in medical ethics and by a consultant clinical pharmacologist who is also a general physician in the hospital.

What does the Priorities Forum do?

The Forum has discussed a wide range of clinical issues, relating both to policy and to individual patients. The way it functions has evolved through developing 'case law'. Some of the elements of this approach are:

- involvement of clinicians,
- an ethical framework,
- communication.

These elements are described below using examples of the workings of the Forum.

Involving clinicians

A major role of the Forum is to provide clinical advice to the HA. A key element is the involvement of clinicians. Clinicians are given guidance before attending the Forum, which essentially asks them three questions:

Question 1: *Your service has a fixed envelope of resource. If you want to do something different, can it be done by substituting a treatment of lower value?*

This can result in a substitution of treatments. For example, when the dermatologists asked for resources to pay for isoretinoin (a drug used to treat severe acne) they agreed, after long discussions with the Forum, they would no longer refer patients for electrolysis but use the resources to treat severe acne sufferers.

Question 2: *If demand for your service is increasing, what criteria are you using to agree the threshold of treatment?*

This question may be answered by reference to national or locally agreed guidelines. One example of the use of explicit guidelines are the criteria for the renal replacement programme. The Forum agreed to support the criteria presented to them by the clinical director of the renal unit, that patients should receive renal replacement therapy on the following conditions: if they wish to receive treatment, and if they are likely to survive out of hospital for longer than three months, irrespective of age but taking into account cerebral function.

Another example is the guidelines for referral for coronary angiography. In this instance, because more people were receiving angiography in the local hospital than were covered by the annual contract, the money allocated by the HA was insufficient to meet demand. Criteria were agreed which meant that the clinical need of the patients who would be treated was greater than before.

In both cases, the criteria limited the availability of potential treatment for some patients, who, if there had been more resources available, might have benefited. The purpose of discussion at the Forum was to be open and explicit about this.

Another example of where the Forum provided the opportunity to be open about difficulties faced by a service was in response to social service cuts in child and adolescent mental health. The clinical director came to the Forum to highlight the impact of social services cuts on child and adolescent services. She proposed guidelines, which made it explicit what the criteria for referral would be; she also made it explicit that certain groups of children and young people would not be offered assessment or treatment. It would no longer be possible to offer a service to children without a definable and treatable psychiatric disorder, a category including many children with school-based behaviour problems and children whose disturbance reflected inadequate parenting, care and social support. By accepting these criteria the Forum openly recognised that treatment would be denied to some, and resources would be diverted to more seriously disturbed children for whom effective medical interventions were available.

Question 3: *If you do not believe that it is possible either to draw thresholds for care or to substitute treatment, then which service might you give a smaller envelope of resource to in order for you to enlarge yours?*

This question of choice between treatments is extremely difficult. Experience shows that it is very difficult to elicit a response from clinicians and to withdraw a service. When the services within a particular Trust were reviewed, the savings identified from ceasing to carry them out were small. It was rarely possible to agree to stop a whole service because there are always patients who might benefit and the concept of relative priority is difficult to quantify.

The proposal to close some community hospitals in the county is an illustration of the difficulty of trying to stop a service. This provoked widespread public objection and in the consultation there have been no proposals put forward for alternative cuts. The only solution suggested has been that the government should give the county more resources. Although we might agree with this point of view, the need to prioritise remains.

Making a decision whether to share out resources or to restrict trreatment is difficult, particularly when it is on behalf of other people. It is easier to choose when there is some resource available, even between two or more competing demands. For example, the Forum was asked to make a choice about whether an additional £100,000 should be spent on more beta-interferon, cataract operations or cochlear implants. Essentially this meant making a choice between

1 a drug which, for certain patients with multiple sclerosis, will improve quality of life. Cost: £8–10,000 a year per patient.
2 an effective operation which enables people to retain independent living within the community. Cost: £723 per cataract operation.
3 an operation which enables people to hear, improving communication and allowing integration of children into mainstream schooling. Cost: £25,000 for the first year and £2,000 for subsequent years.

The money available could only partially meet the demand in all cases. In the end, 50 per cent went to more cataract operations and 50 per cent to fund two further cochlear implants.

There are difficulties in making such decisions about who should be treated. This was a choice between treatments all of which improved quality of life rather than meeting urgent need. Even so it was hard to decide exactly who should be treated. Even more difficult are decisions between treatments that could save life, albeit for a short period, and treatments that could improve quality of life over a longer period. Generic measures such as QALYs can be of some guidance but they do not provide the answers.

Whatever decision is made, some people lose out. The HA outlook is based on the utilitarian principle of greatest good for the greatest number. An individual may well be disadvantaged by this approach since his or her needs may be sacrificed for the greater good. Bearing in mind inevitable conflicts of interest, how can we be sure that as a HA we are doing the best job we can in ensuring maximum health benefit for our population?

Ethical framework

Although clinical advice was necessary to identify the issues for discussion, clinicians were not asked to make the judgements. This was the Forum's responsibility. From the beginning, it was apparent that discussions about what should or should not be funded needed to be based on shared values. These were identified by a subgroup of the main Forum who developed an ethical framework, which was formally adopted by the HA, and to which its decisions could be referred.

In setting its ethical framework the group looked at what has been done in other countries and concluded that nobody has the answer. Since there was no formulaic approach, we focused on procedural justice, making sure we were open and explicit. Some key points from the group discussions included:

- Priority-setting is complex and problematic and there is no universal model for success.
- Decisions cannot simply be made on scientific or technical grounds, although these disciplines can help.
- Agreement tends to be about easy options.
- It is often difficult to translate principles into practice when it comes to individual patients.
- Mechanisms need to be developed to draw both experts and the public into the process.
- Choices between clinical areas are difficult to make because there is no common currency.

As a result of these discussions, the subgroup proposed to the HA that the ethical framework to guide its decisions should be based on: effectiveness, equity and patient choice.[1]

Effectiveness

Effectiveness is the extent to which a treatment or other health care intervention achieves a desired effect (notably the proportion of patients who would be expected to show the effect).

The Forum considers evidence of effectiveness from research, placing emphasis on results of randomised controlled trials and on the strength of the evidence available. QALYs, Numbers Needed to Treat, Years of Life Gained and median life expectancy are all taken into account where appropriate.

When considering effectiveness, three questions apply:

- *Is there good evidence that this treatment is effective?*
  Treatments shown to be highly effective should be funded depending on the value that is placed on them. The value placed on the effect is a judgement as to how valuable that effect is to the relevant individual patient compared with the value of other treatments. A treatment that saves the life of young adults and restores them to full fitness is of high value. A treatment that removes a slight blemish from an unexposed part of the body would normally be of low value. The impact of an effective treatment also needs to be considered. By impact we mean the value of an effect weighted for the degree of effectiveness. A treatment may be highly effective, for example extending life of 90 per cent of people with a certain terminal illness by two days, but its impact would be considered small because such an extension of life is considered unimportant by most people.
- *Is there good evidence that this treatment is not effective?*
  When there is no evidence of effectiveness the treatments should not be funded.
- *Is there no good evidence either way?*
  Many treatments fall into the indeterminate category. It may be that what evidence there is is not good because there have not been any well-designed large trials. Large well-designed trials provide very good quality evidence of the effectiveness of an intervention. Anecdotal evidence from a small number of clinicians is, in general, poor evidence. Between these extremes there is a broad spectrum of evidence of varying quality. Even methodologically rigorous trials may fail to provide good evidence because, for example, the outcome measures used do not include outcomes critical to the questions of priority, or because the population studied is different from that of concern to the HA. Also, much existing good practice is not based on research evidence but on observed outcomes. Overemphasis on evidence from clinical trials can bias care towards drugs and acute interventions because trials in areas such as mental health and social care are more difficult to undertake.

Thus the following principles apply when there is no good evidence:

- There is no policy not to fund such treatments.
- A treatment should not be given low priority simply on the grounds that there is no good evidence for it.

Equity

The HA has agreed that commitment to equity in access to health care requires certain things:

> No patient or group of patients should be treated differently from any other group of patients suffering to a similar degree from the same condition. There should be no discrimination on grounds of employment status, family circumstances, lifestyle, learning difficulty, age, race, sex, social position, financial status, religion or place of abode.

The justification for this principle is that, given the difficulty of making generalisations about the effect of any condition on the well-being of different people, the fairest principle is one of non-discrimination. This is also in line with the moral principle underlying NHS provision that every person counts as much as any other.

Equity requires that health care be allocated fairly and justly and on the basis of need. There are two senses of need:

Urgent: for example, a person injured in a road traffic accident;

Lifetime health need: for example, treatment for acne to avoid disfigurement or providing a hearing aid to improve the quality of life. Lifetime health need is based on the concept of well-being. Priority should be given to all those who are worst off in relation to lifetime well-being. Whether those who are worst off might or might not be said to be responsible for their position is not a relevant consideration. It is not relevant, for example, to smoking-related illnesses. However, it is important that not taking responsibility into account in allocation of health care should sit alongside a health education policy of encouraging citizens to take some responsibility for maintaining their health through a healthy lifestyle or in their behaviour. Environments should be created that assist individuals in health choices and in preventing illness.

Patient choice

The third element of the ethical framework is patient choice. In a culture that encourages patient involvement and in which individuals are increasingly well informed about the treatment options available to them, it is important to be open and honest with the public.

The commitment to patient choice does not mean that if an individual requests a certain treatment the HA will purchase it. We would not make an exception to a decision not to purchase an intervention simply for that reason. If an intervention is not purchased because it is not sufficiently effective then it would be inequitable to purchase it simply because a patient wants it, thereby reducing the funds to help others.

However, there are three important areas where patient choice is an important consideration. First, in assessing research on the effectiveness of a treatment, it is important that the outcome measures used in the research include those which matter to patients. The Forum encourages research which ensures the patients' views about the relevant outcomes are taken into account.

Second, within interventions that are purchased, patients should be able to make their own choices about the interventions they are to have. The provision of information and the fostering of clinical relationships that support patients in coming to their own decisions is encouraged by the Forum

Third, each patient is unique. Flexibility is needed to allow exceptions to the general decision not to purchase where there is reason to believe that a particular patient may gain significantly from a particular treatment. (Exceptions are not allowed simply in response to someone's personal desire.)

This ethical framework is the basis of our approach to making decisions about priorities within the county. However, it does not stand in isolation. Other factors have to be considered, such as national priorities and directives, and the overall financial situation within the district. Further work is being done to align financial decisions with the principles of the framework.

Communication

The Forum discusses priorities with the support of clinicians using the ethical framework as a guide, but discussions are to no avail if they are not communicated. There are a variety of audiences who need to know the outcomes of decisions. These include clinicians in both primary and secondary care, managers within the Trusts and the HA, and most important, the public. Since the Forum is a representational body it is assumed that the decisions made are taken back to the various participating groups – an assumption that is not always correct! The main methods of communication are:

- 'lavender' statements (so called because of their colour) which are sent to all GPs and trusts to inform them of decisions;
- regular reports to the HA, of all meetings and decisions as well as special events such as seminars;
- reinforcement via other routes, for example a prescribing news-letter which goes to all GPs;
- publicity via the Department of Public Health annual report;
- the CHC public health group, which is increasingly involved with the public.

One of the unique features of the Priorities Forum are the lavender statements which are produced and ratified by the Forum before being sent to every GP practice and Trust. Lavender statements have been produced for a wide range of topics. They have covered aspects of the work of the Forum such as screening, prevention, new drugs, research, specialist services and national policy and wherever possible they reflect the ethical framework.

For example, prior to the national guidance, the media raised expectations about the benefits of prostatic specific antigen screen-ing for all men. The Forum considered the evidence and sent out the statement advising against such an approach:

> OHA has considered the evidence for the benefits that could be achieved by the screening for prostatic cancer and has concluded that there is at present no justification for intro-ducing a population screening programme. This applies to whichever of the tests currently available for screening is used – digital rectal examination, transrectal ultrasound or prostatic specific antigen.

Initially there had been some nervousness about explicit statements such as this. But GPs have welcomed the lavender statements as sup-portive, enabling them to justify difficult decisions to their patients. In general, this has been county-wide advice.

There is always a tension between the present and the future, between prevention with its benefits down the track and treatment now. As a district we agreed that consistent advice was needed on the prescription of statins (drugs which lower levels of blood cholesterol and thereby prevent coronary heart disease and its complications). The Forum considered effectiveness and equity as important criteria in providing guidance. Awareness of the potential cost to the health care system came into the debate, and there was general support for investment in prevention. Arguments that the needs of those with existing heart disease should take precedence were not raised, an implicit acceptance of the value of prevention.

Introducing new drugs can be problematic and the clinical pharmacologist supporting the work of the Forum has devised a framework which allows comparisons of effectiveness between different groups of drugs, for example drugs which are life-saving versus those which improve quality of life. Application of this framework led to the advice in the Appendix to this chapter, about the new drug for motor neurone disease, Riluzole, which was felt to be of insufficient effectiveness for it to be allocated additional resources.

Since the environment in which we are working is one in which there is a high level of research activity, it has been necessary to make it clear, via lavender statements, what the boundaries are between Health Service activity and research activity. This can be confusing to patients who hear of a research trial, want to be included, but the design precludes it. This is compounded by the media who report miracle cures where the research evidence is insufficient to support the additional funding needed to procure the treatment. Headlines such as 'I can live again' as a result of surgery for Parkinson's disease led to a lavender statement:

> it is not at present possible for OHA to fund stereotactic surgery for tremor, including that for Parkinsonism. An initial discussion has been held at the Priorities Forum, but the Forum is not yet convinced that the effectiveness of the treatment is sufficient as to justify purchasing it.

The strength of research evidence underpins other decisions by the authority when the Forum wishes to see a change in existing commitment of resources. A critical review of the evidence of new drugs for cancer convinced the Forum that the resources for oncology needed to be increased to allow cancer patients effective treatment. This was in line with local views and national policy on improving cancer services. However, it is often not as simple as saying that we will not fund treatments which are not in research trials. One example the Forum considered was intravascular coils, a potentially life-saving treatment for people with intracranial bleeds (a form of stroke that can result in death or disability).

Research was funded for one type of bleed but it was apparent that the coils were also effective for another type of bleed, in some patients who would previously not have had a treatment available to them. The neuroradiologists argued that it was unethical to deny these patients the option of treatment although they could not be included in the study because of its design. A compromise was reached on treatment for these patients.

Increasingly the Forum seeks to reflect some of the broader dimensions of health. There have been discussions about the interface with social care, which have demonstrated how difficult it can be to share values across different organisational cultures. Increasingly, the Forum will be engaged in closer working with other sectors, particularly with the development of the Health Improvement Programmes.[2] This will bring with it a need to move towards an identification of shared values, values which reflect those of local communities.

The HA, and primary care groups (PCGs)[3] need to continue to respond to government priorities, in particular initiatives to reduce social inequalities, thereby reducing health inequalities. A recent review of the evidence about nicotine replacement therapy (NRT) has shown that it is highly effective in helping people stopping smoking, yet it is currently not available on NHS prescription. One of the recommendations from the national expert advisory committee was that NRT should be made available on prescription, since this would improve access to an effective measure to reduce smoking for those in lower income groups and help address the government's concerns about current health inequalities. The Forum supported this recommendation and is seeking ways to introduce NRT and target it at the more deprived parts of the county, where smoking rates are highest.

Finally, there are two areas which still require particular consideration: involving the public and ensuring accountability; and the current structural and political changes.

Meaningful public involvement has been under consideration for some time, but is a difficult area. On the advice of the CHC a leaflet has been produced that describes the process of the Priorities Forum, including the ethical framework. Initial discussions have intimated that procedural justice – reassuring the public about the values behind and processes of decision-making – is the major concern. Can the HA answer the question – are you being fair? In future it is proposed to issue press briefings and increase the public awareness of the work of the Forum. The appeal process which exists for individuals to challenge the decisions of the Forum will also be publicised.

A second challenge is the structural changes occurring from Labour government policy. Ethical issues will need to be considered by PCGs as they take on a greater role in deciding the shape of local services. The Regional Specialist Commissioning Groups need to consider the principles on which they base decisions on available health care for larger populations – for example for the introduction of new cancer drugs or appropriate levels of renal replacement therapy. The ethical framework adopted by the county will need to reflect these changes. Another consideration will be the work of the National Institute of Clinical Excellence (NICE).[4] Its role will be to give guidance for effective practice. What is unclear is the extent to which this will mean adopting explicit national criteria for prioritisation. Historically, national guidance has been based on clinical effectiveness. What is needed is a national framework for prioritisation which reflects national values.

The Forum needs to adapt to meet these changes, but will continue to have a role in steering health policy in Oxfordshire.

Notes

The Priorities Forum would not have been possible without the dedication and commitment of its members, in particular Tony Hope, Tom Jones, Paul Brankin, Penny Thewlis, Vivyenne Rubinstein, Roger Crisp, John Reynolds, Ruth Kipping and Alan Web.

1 Tony Hope.
2 Health Improvement Programmes are multi-agency plans for improving the health of the community which are signed up to by all partners, but written on their behalf by Health Authorities in England and Wales.
3 PCGs (primary care groups) are groups of general practices, covering between 60 and 200,000 patients, who share administrative and organisational boundaries.
4 This is a new national body in the NHS, which will co-ordinate efforts to promote clinical effectiveness.

APPENDIX: AN EXAMPLE OF A PRIORITIES FORUM POLICY STATEMENT

Number: 9

Subject: Riluzole

Date of decision/meeting: 26 September 1996

POLICY

Riluzole, which became licensed for UK use in August 1996, is the first drug that has been found to influence the course of motor neurone disease, but it does not arrest the disease process. Trials show that it prolongs median life expectation from diagnosis in sufferers from the disease by 3 months compared with placebo. The incidence of adverse effects is higher than with placebo, and patients taking it experience no functional improvements. The cost of treating one patient for a year with Riluzole 50 mg bd is £3,700.

In the light of the existing knowledge and experience of the drug, Oxfordshire Health Authority considers it to be of low priority and will not normally purchase it at present.

There is no regulation preventing GPs from prescribing it, but Oxfordshire Health Authority's advice is that because of this policy they should not do so. No special allowance will be made for the drug in GP drug budgets except in the case of patients already established on it before this Policy Statement was agreed, usually as a result of participation in a pre-licensing trial.

4

USING A CITIZENS' JURY TO INVOLVE THE PUBLIC IN A DECISION ABOUT PRIORITIES: A CASE STUDY

Gill Needham

This chapter describes the experience of one health authority in England – Buckinghamshire – which involved a citizens' jury in an important decision about the development of services for people with back pain.

Citizens' juries

Citizens' juries are 'small groups of citizens, selected to represent the general public rather than any interest or sector, who meet to deliberate upon a policy question. They are informed about the issue, take evidence from the witnesses and cross-examine them, then discuss the matter amongst themselves and reach a decision'.[1] The concept has been developed during the 1980s and 1990s by Peter Dienl at the University of Wuppertal in Germany and Ned Crosby of the Jefferson Center, Minneapolis, in the USA. Its application to public involvement in health policy in the NHS is currently under scrutiny. The first citizens' jury to be used in this way in Britain was organised by Cambridge and Huntingdon Health Authority in March 1996. The main advantage of the citizens' jury compared to other methods is its degree of sophistication. Juries usually 'sit' for four or five days, during which time they are given background information and explanation and then evidence from a series of witnesses, with adequate time for questioning and debate before they reach a decision about their final recommendations. This perhaps stands up to criticisms of health authorities' public involvement work as 'the unaccountable in pursuit of the uninformed'.[2]

Background: Public involvement in Buckinghamshire Health Authority

The health authority had previous experience of and considerable commitment to involving the public in its decision making. The 1996 Communications Strategy[3] launched a programme of work:

> During 1996/7 a framework for public involvement will be established which will enable the Authority to use established structures and methods for involving the public. This framework will operate at different levels. Some methods will lead to information being fed directly into the authority, others will feed into local providers; others will be based within primary care. Once these have been developed, they will be available as tools to be utilised for particular subject matters.
>
> (p. 12)

Improving services for people with back pain

Buckinghamshire Health Authority identified the management of back pain as a key area in its 1996/7 corporate contract. The authority had an ongoing programme of work entitled GRiPP (Getting Research into Practice and Purchasing), which involved working with local clinicians in primary and secondary care, and with others, to identify a topic of local importance, consider the latest research evidence and develop and disseminate local consensus of good practice, often in the form of clinical guidelines or public education materials. The Local Medical Committee approached the health authority to carry out such a project on back pain. It is the second most common reason for referring patients from primary to secondary care and some GPs had expressed concern about aspects of the services available locally.

In 1994 the Clinical Standards Advisory Group (CSAG) published a long-awaited review of the epidemiology of back pain[4] and the latest evidence of the effectiveness of available treatments. The estimates in this review suggested that the cost of back pain to the NHS in Buckinghamshire was at least £5.5 million annually. This did not take into the account the financial, social and psychological costs of back pain to the sufferers themselves and the costs to local employers. In addition, many back pain sufferers were known to turn to the private sector for treatment, perhaps because they preferred private health care but also, in many cases, because certain treatments like osteopathy and chiropractic were not available locally within the NHS. Indeed, evidence cited in the CSAG review suggested that these treatments are clinically effective and CSAG recommended that purchasers consider their use. In a county like Buckinghamshire, which is relatively affluent but has a number of areas of deprivation, this posed an important question about equity of access to effective treatments.

The authority therefore embarked on a major piece of work to consider how services for people with back pain might be improved. As part of the public involvement strategy it was committed to involving both patients and the public from an early stage in assessing the implications of current evidence of the effectiveness of treatments which were purchased and those which were not. This is particularly important in the case of treatments like physiotherapy and osteopathy, where patients' values and experiences are key factors alongside 'scientific' evidence of clinical effectiveness.

King's Fund citizens' juries project

It was particularly opportune that at the time of these discussions the King's Fund announced that it had established a grants programme to 'evaluate the potential of citizens' juries as a means of public consultation within health authorities'.[5] Health authorities were invited to submit bids for projects to set up citizens' juries on specific topics.

This presented an ideal opportunity to help forward an important project while simultaneously testing a new and exciting method of public involvement. An outline proposal was duly submitted to the King's Fund and this was ultimately successful. The Buckinghamshire citizens' jury project was to be a collaborative one with a stakeholder steering group playing a major role. In order to establish a broad ownership of the project, this group comprised representatives of every directorate of the health authority, a manager from a local Trust, a GP, a Community Health Council representative and two representatives from the local branch of the Back Pain Association. After some discussion the group agreed the objective for the project:

To consult the public in order to help the health authority identify the best package of services for people with back pain.

The question

One of the most crucial aspects of a citizens' jury is the selection of the question which they will address. This has to be clear and focused and be one for which sufficient evidence can be presented by witnesses in the time-scale to allow an informed discussion and recommendations. Initially the group's suggestion was:

What kind of care should the health authority purchase for people with back pain?

with the additional reminder that resources are limited. After some discussion it became clear that this question was too broad and too open-ended. In order to answer it, the jury would have to receive evidence about every possible element of services for back pain. It was also likely to produce recommendations which were so general that it would be difficult for the health authority to identify the influence on their decision-making. As the discussion unfolded it became evident that the major issue was one of equity. Public and professionals were both concerned that people in Buckinghamshire with back pain were increasingly using the private sector. They did so because this was the only access to osteopaths and chiropractors who seemed, anecdotally, to have more success in reducing their pain and helping them become mobile again. This system automatically excluded those unable or unwilling to pay from receiving supposedly effective treatment. The question for the jury then became:

Should Buckinghamshire Health Authority purchase services from osteopaths and chiropractors for people with moderate/severe back pain?

There was still a problem with this version. Most people, faced with this question, which appeared to be simply suggesting an extension of the choice of services currently available, would automatically answer in the affirmative. In fact the situation was more complex. In the current climate of resource constraints, the only way in which funding could possibly be identified for purchasing something 'new' was by shifting resources from elsewhere. The area of treatment corresponding most closely to osteopathy and chiropractic is physiotherapy, purchasing the one would inevitably reduce the use of the other. The question was therefore supplemented as follows:

> If yes, given that (a) these services are not currently purchased by the Health Authority and (b) no extra resources are available for back pain services, should some of the money we currently spend on physiotherapy be spent on osteopathy and chiropractic?

Developing the jury's agenda

The task for the jury was to weigh up a complex range of evidence on back pain services including evidence of clinical effectiveness of different treatments, experience and preferences of patients, experience and views of a range of key professionals (some, perhaps, with vested interests), financial considerations and health policy. To support this process, what kinds of witness would be required to give a balance of appropriate evidence? This is very important because of the potential for manipulation of the jury by witness selection. This was the group's choice:

- people with back pain: more than one to reflect different experiences of treatments and services (two sufferers recruited through the local Back Pain Association; one had achieved success through NHS treatment, the other had used private treatment);
- someone who could talk about the research evidence about back pain treatments (a reviewer from the Cochrane Back Pain Group);
- a local GP with a particular interest in back pain;
- a physiotherapist, an orthopaedic surgeon, an osteopath and a chiropractor;
- the Back Pain Association (a national officer, dealing with enquiries from the public);
- purchasers (the Director of Public Health and the Director of Finance);
- providers (a Trust Director of Finance).

The practitioners (the osteopath, chiropractor and physiotherapist) were recruited nationally via their professional organisations. It was felt that local practitioners would have too direct an interest in the question. Successful recruitment and briefing of witnesses was crucial to the process. They needed to adhere to their brief, speak clearly and answer questions honestly. One concern was that more charismatic witnesses would carry more weight. In the event jurors were able to distinguish between content and presentation. Witnesses took their responsibilities very seriously, were well prepared and obeyed their brief.

It was also felt that the jurors should be given written background information. This had to be as objective and free of bias as possible. It would cover the following:

- current service provision for back pain for Buckinghamshire residents;
- epidemiology of back pain in Buckinghamshire;
- mechanisms for allocating/redirecting resources;
- clinical (and cost) effectiveness of different therapies;
- estimated expenditure on back pain, public and private (including pain relief);
- feedback on local back pain services/provision;
- statistics of use of alternative practitioners in Buckinghamshire.

Efforts were made to ensure that the information was clear and well presented. It was all tested with a focus group and amendments made accordingly. A glossary was included. The jury could request any further information at any time during the proceedings.

Selection of the jurors

One common criticism of citizens' juries is that the juries are 'not representative of the local population'. In this case, up to sixteen jurors were required, to represent the population of the county of Buckinghamshire. The King's Fund stipulated that the selection of jurors should be carried out by an organisation independent of the health authority. A market research company was therefore commissioned to select the sixteen as a quota sample to reflect the population breakdown in terms of the following variables:

- geographical location;
- urban or rural;
- gender;
- age;
- ethnicity;
- employment status.

The only group to be excluded were elected representatives (parliamentary or local government). It was decided not to select by sending letters to a sample from the electoral register, as this might bias the sample to those sufficiently motivated to send a reply. Instead the company was asked to identify the quota by knocking on doors and pavement canvassing.

The market research company recruited sixteen jurors. The age and sex profile was as shown in the table.

	18–24	25–44	45–64	65+	Total
Males	2	1	4	1	8
Females	0	4	3	1	8

One male in the 18–24 age band withdrew because of a last-minute holiday plan. The fifteen remaining jurors attended throughout. There was in fact a gap between the youngest member, 18, and the next, who was 31. This showed up a problem that all citizens' juries have experienced – that of recruiting young people in their twenties. Half of the jurors were recruited from urban areas of the county and half from rural. There was a reasonable socio-economic mix: a motor mechanic, a publican, a fire officer, a pharmacist, a computer programmer, a housewife, and others. Jurors were paid £200 each for attending and their travel and caring expenses were also paid.

The company reported some problems with the recruitment: many people declined because one of the jury days happened to be Mothers' Day, young people were reluctant to give up a weekend, working people were not easily able to take the two days off work. The choice of days – a weekend and two week days – attempted to take these issues into account but future juries would need to experiment with different configurations of days.

Just a PR exercise

One of the King's Fund's criteria for allocating the grants was that the health authority should demonstrate commitment to taking account of the jury's recommendations. Without this commitment, the citizens' jury becomes an elaborate public relations exercise, thus discrediting the methodology. This was discussed with the chairman, chief executive and other directors at Buckinghamshire Health Authority. While it was impossible for them to promise unconditionally to adopt any forthcoming recommendations, they did agree that the recommendations would be discussed at the next authority meeting (with the jurors present and with speaking rights) and then become part of the annual discussions on the Purchasing Plan (which incorporates changes to be made for the following year). If, after the consultation process, changes were to be made, these would take place from the following April.

The role of the facilitators

Facilitators are pivotal to the jury process. They are the guardians of the process, ensuring that the jury members are able to complete their task, while at the same time supporting the needs of each individual juror. There has been considerable discussion in the literature on citizens' juries of their role and the skills required. The King's Fund selected their own two facilitators for all three of the juries they funded. Both had considerable experience of working in the NHS as well as being experienced facilitators with a particular commitment to 'public involvement' work. They worked as a team with specific, complementary roles which were made clear to the jurors at the outset. The first facilitator's role was to chair the proceedings and to help the jurors achieve their task of asking the questions. He kept everyone to time, introduced the witnesses and ensured that questions were answered. The second facilitator's role was called 'the jurors' friend'; she ensured that the jurors felt comfortable, that they were able to make their views heard and that they were happy with the way the process was managed. She led all the *in camera* sessions.

The observers

In the United States, citizens' juries are observed by large numbers of people (up to a hundred). Although it is important that the jury process is open to scrutiny, this has been kept to a minimum in the UK juries, to avoid the 'goldfish bowl' effect for jurors. A policy for observers was therefore drawn up and agreed by the steering group. Observers had to be managed. Guidelines for their conduct were drawn up so that they would not interfere with the jury process. They were segregated from the jurors, as were the witnesses. It was important to ask the jurors the extent to which they were distracted by the observers, of whom there could be up to sixteen in the room at any one time.

Establishing ground rules and agreeing objectives

Getting any disparate group of people to work together is challenging, and particularly so when such a demanding task is required of them. This necessitated some intensive preparatory work with the facilitators. This began on the first morning with a long session *in camera* where jurors negotiated the ground rules for how they hoped to work during the four days. They spent some time discussing what made group work successful and what made it fail. They also spent time discussing their objectives: what they hoped to achieve by the final session.

Both the ground rules and objectives were revisited daily. Each day began with an *in camera* session, where the previous day was reviewed and any problems discussed. Similarly at the end of each day jurors were encouraged to say how they were feeling about the process. The facilitators also spoke to jurors individually. Jurors initially expressed anxiety; this seemed to reduce during the four days.

Taking evidence

The jury had some preparation for the majority of witnesses; they had the opportunity to read the handouts in advance and in a preparatory session with the facilitators discussed the information they hoped to gain from each. The witness slots had a standard format, with the facilitators creating an informal atmosphere. The witness was introduced and then spoke for around fifteen minutes (none exceeded their time limit). Jurors were then invited to ask any quick questions for clarification; in most cases there were three or four of these. The jury then split into small groups of three or four and spent up to ten minutes planning the questions they would like to ask the witness. Each group then had the opportunity to ask two questions. This technique worked well as all the questions were thoughtful and perceptive.

The facilitators changed the seating position of the jurors daily so that they would work in different groups. They spent considerable time planning this as soon as it became evident which jurors were more likely to be quiet and would need some encouragement to participate.

Deliberation and decision-making

How do the jurors in a citizens' jury weigh up the evidence, deliberate and finally reach a decision? At the end of the penultimate day the jurors discussed how they would approach the task. In negotiation they agreed that any minority positions would be acknowledged and reported.

On the final morning there was some tension. The facilitators' input was crucial in reassuring them that they would be supported in the decision-making process. The morning session was devoted to the three extra witnesses requested by the jury to help them in their task. The first was a recalled witness – the Director of Public Health – who was asked to supply more information about the quality of local physiotherapy services and also to discuss the funding of research and development in the NHS. The second was an occupational health specialist called to talk about the impact of back pain in the workplace and potential preventive strategies. The final and key witness was the Head of Therapy Services from a Yorkshire Trust who had integrated osteopaths into her department to work alongside physiotherapists in providing services for people with back pain.

For the rest of the day, jurors worked in three groups to agree on their guiding principles, the recommendations and the concerns they wished to express to the health authority. The jurors presented their recommendations to the chief executive at the end of the afternoon.

The recommendations

The jurors first listed their underlying principles:

- informed patient choice;
- early assessment and access to treatment;
- importance of the gatekeeping role;
- a service available to everyone who needs it;
- the need to take the onus away from the GP by the development of guidelines about the management of back pain;
- the need to better use existing resources and to identify alternative sources of funding;
- the need to reduce waiting time for diagnosis and treatment at each stage in the process.

They then outlined their vision:

An integrated system for back pain based on early referral to a centre of excellence, with joint education and practice development. This would be supported by the use of guidelines in primary care, professional development and evidence-based practice, and underpinned by collaboration and public education in awareness about back pain.

A summary of the jurors' recommendations is reproduced here.

To improve patient choice
In the next year the health authority should:

- Set up meetings with GP representatives to discuss and agree guidelines for an early diagnosis and referral system, with referral within two weeks of seeing the GP.
- Use these meetings to investigate the potential for establishing local back pain clinics similar to those at Barnsley or Marylebone.

In the longer term, the health authority should:

- Negotiate with physiotherapists to ensure their agreement to work with osteopaths and chiopractors.
- Initiate discussions with osteopathy and chiropractic organisations about local co-operation.
- Ensure that therapists within back pain clinics offer patients verbal and written information (such as the 'Back book') about back pain and its management.

To better utilise public funds and resources
In the next year, the health authority should:

- Conduct a feasibility study into the possibility of establishing a pilot project on the use of chiropractors and osteopaths in back pain clinics.
- Investigate the cost implications of such a pilot project.
- Investigate the cost implications of educating and raising the awareness of GPs and physiotherapists about the pilot project.
- Implement a steering group to establish a pilot project.
- Establish links with other relevant bodies and interest groups to forward the pilot project.
- Look at funding for the pilot project through savings made by the adoption of guidelines (e.g. savings in use of outpatient clinics or X-rays).
- Investigate alternative sources of funding from industry, the NHS Research and Development budget and the Social Security budget savings to finance back pain clinics in the longer term.

- Explore the possibility of introducing chiropractors and osteopaths into existing physiotherapy departments by transferring funding from physiotherapy posts as staff leave or through increased funding.
- Begin pilot projects on cross-training between physiotherapists, osteopaths, chiropractors and GPs.
- Enhance public and professional understanding of the number of back pain sufferers and the extent of the problem.

In the longer term, the health authority should:

- Conduct high-quality research and clinical audit into the use of chiropractors and osteopaths in NHS back pain clinics, including monitoring and reviewing these services.
- Ensure wide implementation of the pilot projects, if they are successful.
- Assess GP and patient satisfaction with the pilot projects.
- Undertake a public awareness campaign about the causes of back pain.

To develop collaboration with and between professionals and practitioners
The health authority should:

- Agree to the development of a centre of excellence for back pain.
- Investigate existing centres of excellence for back pain.
- Set up a multidisciplinary working group to plan and oversee the activities of such a centre.
- Establish and carry out research on:
    how other health authorities have established centres of excellence for back pain;
    potential cost savings of such a centre;
    who might be prepared to financially support the development or running of such a centre.
- Formulate local guidelines for back pain assessment and control.
- Ensure earlier treatment for back pain sufferers to make sure that those with acute pain do not become chronic pain sufferers.

The jurors also asked the health authority to note their concerns that:

- Their opinion might not be taken seriously.
- There might not be a will to change amongst professionals.
- There are myths about medicine that may hinder development.
- Professional bodies might block multidisciplinary working.
- The development of a centre of excellence and the provision of osteopathy and chiropractic within the NHS might cause demand for NHS services to outstrip supply.

● There might not be funds available to set up further, permanent projects based on the pilot projects.

What did the health authority learn from the citizens' jury project?

The lessons and gains from the jury project fall into two distinct categories: outcome and process.

Outcome

The outcome of the jury can be assessed by the quality of the final recommendations and their usefulness to the health authority. To what extent does public involvement add value to decision-making? The jurors were quick to realise that the decision they had been asked to make could not easily be taken in isolation. They therefore decided to make the question more specific and to relate it to possible treatment for back pain sufferers in Buckinghamshire. The resulting recommendations were more useful than anything envisaged. They have forced the authority to take a longer-term view but given a framework for experimentation and evaluation as well as education and development. The key recommendations from the jury have subsequently formed part of an ongoing back pain project, with members of the jury involved in the project team. Problems might have arisen had the recommendations proved unacceptable to the authority. As it is the jurors have been frustrated by the length of time taken to embark on any form of implementation. It might be argued that it would be unethical to allow fifteen people to invest four days in a potentially fruitless exercise.

Process

Health authority staff involved in this project learned considerably from the process. There was initial scepticism and a concern that a group of 'ordinary people' would be unable to understand the complex issues involved. In the event staff were pleasantly surprised; once the jurors were given the language and concepts of, say, clinical effectiveness they were perfectly able to make sense of the arguments and questioned the witnesses with great perception. This was an important lesson for the staff, as public servants, about sharing information and hence power with their users, rather than hiding behind the mystique of technical language.

If some health authority staff had preconceived ideas about the jurors, the jurors similarly brought along their own image of the health authority; the majority knew very little about its role and were presumably influenced by an often critical local press. Time was invested on the opening evening session in breaking down some of these barriers. The health authority and the jurors had to trust and respect each other if the project was to succeed. The relationship which developed was a considerable achievement in a short time.

Notes

1 Stewart, J., Kendall, E. and Coote, A., *Citizens' Juries*, London: Institute for Public Policy Research, 1994.
2 Pfeffer, N. and Pollock, A., 'Public opinion and the NHS', *British Medical Journal* 307 (25 Sept. 1993), pp. 750–1.
3 This is the contract which every health authority has to agree with its NHS Executive Regional Office to specify the work it will complete in the year. The authority's performance is monitored against the contract (Buckinghamshire Health Authority 1996 Communications Strategy, internal document).
4 Clinical Standards Advisory Group, *Back Pain: Report of a CSAG Committee on Back Pain*, London: HMSO, 1994.
5 Elizabeth, Susan, 'Introduction', in S. Davies, S. Elizabeth, B. Hanley, B. New and B. Sang, *Ordinary Wisdom: Reflections on an Experiment in Citizenship and Health*, London: King's Fund, 1998, p. 1.

5

INTERNATIONAL PERSPECTIVES ON PRIORITY-SETTING IN HEALTH CARE

Louise Locock

Introduction

International interest in health care priority-setting or rationing has been growing, yet the kind of approaches adopted and the values underlying them differ substantially. Health care rationing is one example of how political choices vary between countries. This chapter looks at approaches to priority-setting in several countries, and explores the different ethical assumptions underlying these approaches. In most political systems, an equitable distribution of resources is a stated policy goal. How, then, do they arrive at such different positions?

One answer is that societies have different and competing understandings of what constitutes equity in distributing resources. These competing views in turn depend largely on the relative importance attached to the three principles of liberty, equality and social solidarity. In practice these principles may conflict with each other, and in reaching judgements about the distribution of resources, nations are making different trade-offs between them. In doing so, they may also define them differently. Varying interpretations within one principle may be as significant in understanding the choices made as trade-offs between principles.

Liberty, for example, can be 'negative' – the absence of state interference – or it can be more positive freedom, where the state limits some freedoms to ensure greater liberty for all.[1]

Equality can mean equality before the law, equality of political power, of opportunity, of resources and welfare, or equality of freedom. As J. S. Mill comments, agreement on the principle can conceal radically different interpretations in practice.

> Each person maintains that equality is the dictate of justice, except where he thinks that expediency requires inequality. The justice of giving equal protection to the rights of all, is maintained by those who support the most outrageous inequality in the rights themselves.[2]

The values of social solidarity stress the importance of the collective good of the community, rather than individual rights, in reaching decisions about how society should operate. It emphasises the individual's place within a network of social relationships and institutions, and the importance of mutual support within the community. Reducing inequality may be an important strategy for maintaining solidarity.

In making trade-offs, nations are not choosing one principle categorically over the others but rather giving them different emphasis and meaning. Even from these over-simplified accounts it is apparent that there are considerable grey areas between these concepts and that they can be stretched to fit quite different understandings. For example, some would argue liberty has to be curtailed to prevent unacceptable inequalities, in other words that liberty and equality are in some sense opposed to each other. Others would respond that having an equal share in material wealth and political power is a prerequisite for effective freedom, and that liberty and equality are therefore closely related. Nonetheless, the identification of these concepts offers a starting point for understanding why political choices differ.

The Scandinavian approach: equality and social solidarity in priority-setting

Sweden, Norway and Finland are actively engaged in the priority-setting debate. This debate has been open, participative and explicit about resource limitations, with a strong national lead. It is characterised by a belief in egalitarianism, the importance of collective social interests and democratic process. The primary focus here is on Sweden.

Scandinavian egalitarianism is sometimes caricatured by libertarians as stifling individual liberty. In fact the Finnish report on health care describes human dignity, human rights and self-determination as principles which 'require unceasing defending and cherishing', particularly 'in times of crisis, when selfishness easily gains the upper hand and solidarity tends to get forgotten'.[3] Nonetheless, the linkage between human dignity and solidarity in this context is important.

The Swedish priority-setting commission takes a similar approach and proposes the following three basic principles for prioritisation:

HUMAN DIGNITY: every human being has a unique value, and all humans are equally valuable.

NEED or SOLIDARITY: resources should be concentrated where needs are greatest, recognising that needs are not equally distributed and that some illnesses are more amenable to treatment than others. Solidarity requires special attention to the needs of the weakest in society.

EFFICIENCY: when choosing between different measures, 'one should opt, all other things being equal, for that which is most cost-efficient.'[4] In the final report,[5] it is suggested that cost-efficiency can only be applied in comparisons for treating the same disease, as fair comparison of effects between different diseases is impossible. It is *subordinate* to the need and solidarity principles.

The Swedish Commission rejects four other possible principles:

- the *lottery principle*, which would be contrary to the idea of need and solidarity;
- the *demand principle*, which would favour the most eloquent or affluent. Patients 'cannot request treatment which is contrary to science and proven experience' and they have no absolute right to treatment;[6]
- the *benefit principle* (maximising benefit). This could mean spending money on many people with mild disorders to the exclusion of a few seriously ill people, which would conflict with a desire to address health care need and maintain solidarity. (The desire to maximise benefit remains an appropriate principle in decision-making about individual patients, however.)

- the *autonomy principle*, which, whilst valuable in individual care, may conflict with the need and solidarity principle, and should be *subordinate* to it if conflict arises.

Four ethically unacceptable criteria for prioritisation are identified:

- advanced age (except in so far as it affects clinical effectiveness);
- low birth weight (decisions should be individualised, not based on arbitrary limits);
- self-inflicted injuries (although the effect of continuing harmful behaviour may be taken into account in determining likely benefit);
- economic status and social position.

On the basis of its three fundamental principles, the final report[7] proposes that priority-setting at political and administrative level should be guided by the following priority categories:

1 treatment of life-threatening acute and severe chronic diseases; palliative terminal care; treatment of diseases which reduce autonomy;
2 population-based prevention/screening of documented cost-efficiency; individualised prevention and habilitation/rehabilitation;
3 treatment of less severe acute and chronic diseases;
4 'borderline' cases (i.e. unclear whether it is a matter of health or quality of life, e.g. infertility);
5 care for reasons other than disease or injury.

The commission's terms of reference required it to consider formulating a basic or minimum health care package. The commission rejects this approach in both reports, and argues that all the care in groups 1–3, in other words most of the currently provided effective care, should be equitably and collectively funded. It also suggests that group 4 (borderline cases, such as IVF) should be funded if resources are available, and that group 5 should not. (It could perhaps be argued that these recommendations do in fact amount to a recommendation for a minimum package, albeit generously defined.)

The commission is forthright about the relative priority of different principles. The view that human dignity is of primary importance whereas autonomy is not reflects a conception of human dignity founded in social participation and equality. The Scandinavian perception of egalitarianism emphasises its collective, mutual aspect, rather than individual equal rights.

Nonetheless, the ordering of principles at macro-level does not necessarily resolve tensions between them at doctor–patient level. As the commission itself acknowledges, the autonomy and benefit principles play a stronger role in decisions about individual care than they do in the commission's deliberations. The problem in Sweden may be not so much finding national consensus about the principles as turning them into practical decisions. Health care is a powerful symbol of the welfare society in Sweden,[8] and the reality of limits on individual care may be difficult to accept.

This problem underlies a new phase in Scandinavian priority-setting identified by Holm: there is now a move away from the belief that it is possible to devise 'a complete and non-contradictory set of rational decision rules' which will always produce legitimate and rational decisions.[9] Increasingly the focus is on improving the transparency and accountability of the process, rather than the decisions themselves, as the more promising way forward.

Egalitarianism in the Land of the Free: the struggle for universal health care in Oregon, US

The state of Oregon is well known for implementing a systematic policy of explicit rationing by exclusion of particular treatments. Its approach has been extensively analysed.

The US health care system is largely based on private insurance, with a minimum safety net for the very poor (Medicaid) and social insurance for the elderly (Medicare). This reflects the importance attached in the US to individual civil liberties, personal responsibility and enterprise.

Excluding groups of people from care – especially those who cannot afford insurance but who are not poor enough to qualify for Medicaid – is in effect a rationing mechanism. To the extent that these groups have had access to care, it has often been on a charitable, discretionary basis.

This gap in coverage, coupled with spiralling Medicaid costs, prompted the state of Oregon to review its system. In early attempts to limit Medicaid expenditure, a child was refused a bone-marrow transplant operation, and died as a result. The shock caused by this incident led to a fundamental re-examination of the principles of priority-setting, with the aim of establishing 'a publicly defined, standard package of *effective* healthcare (Standard Benefit Package) offered to all Oregonians at an affordable price'.[10]

The Oregon Health Services Commission was appointed to undertake this work. After consulting the local community about their values, and taking expert clinical and economic advice, the commission proposed a ranked list of several hundred condition/treatment pairings, grouped into the following categories:

ESSENTIAL
1 Acute fatal, treatment prevents death and allows full recovery
2 Maternity care, including most new-born disorders
3 Acute fatal, treatment prevents death but does not allow full recovery
4 Preventive care for children
5 Chronic fatal, treatment improves life-span and quality of life
6 Reproductive services, excludes maternity and infertility services
7 Comfort care (palliative care)
8 Preventive dental care, adults and children
9 Proven effective preventive care for adults

VERY IMPORTANT
10 Acute non-fatal, treatment causes return to previous health
11 Chronic non-fatal, one-time treatment improves quality of life
12 Acute non-fatal, treatment without return to previous health
13 Chronic non-fatal, repetitive treatment improves quality of life

VALUABLE TO CERTAIN INDIVIDUALS
14 Acute non-fatal, treatment speeds recovery of self-limiting conditions
15 Infertility services
16 Less effective preventive care for adults
17 Fatal or non-fatal, treatment causes minimal or no improvement in quality of life

The commission recommended to the legislature that the Standard Benefit Package should include all 'essential' services and most 'very important' services. The first list, drawn up in 1990, was never published and contained many errors and counter-intuitive results, such as ranking treatment for thumb-sucking above treatment for AIDS. A revised list, placing greater emphasis on the subjective judgements of members of the commission and less emphasis on cost, was published in 1991 and contained 709 treatment/ condition pairings. Federal approval was originally withheld on the grounds that it discriminated against people with disabilities. Two further revisions were undertaken to accommodate this concern by excluding any considerations of quality of life or the treatment's ability to take the patient to an asymptomatic state of health. The fourth list (with 688 pairings) was accepted in April 1993, and implemented in February 1994.

Although in 1991 the Oregon legislature decided to fund only 587 of the 709 pairings then on the list, it had to vote extra resources to fund this level of service, and the procedures excluded were generally for minor conditions, or treatments with little or no chance of success. For instance, number 709 on the list was life support for anencephalic babies.

The aim of restricting the package for Medicaid recipients was to extend coverage to previously uninsured people, and particularly all people below the federal poverty level. It was also intended to make employment-based insurance covering the same standard package mandatory for all full-time workers and their families. Oregon is therefore trading off existing comprehensiveness for a selected group, in return for new universality.[11] In the other countries considered in this chapter, the question is somewhat different: universality and comprehensiveness are both already established, but can they be maintained? In practice, they may reach the same answer as Oregon: if they want universal access, they may have to sacrifice comprehensive provision.

However, the different starting point in Oregon is crucial in understanding vociferous objections to the plan, which stem from the wider US commitment to civil liberties. At one level the Oregon Plan, in rejecting the right of one section of society to have extensive health care at the expense of others who have no right to health care, is based on egalitarian principles. Yet many critics focus precisely on its *lack* of attention to equal rights and potential discriminatory consequences, 'because it singles out the poor'.[12] There are particular concerns about its unfairness to very poor women, children and elderly people, who previously had a right to comprehensive care under Medicaid, but will now have only restricted access.[13]

The paradox whereby an attempt to improve services for the poor is seen to discriminate against them can perhaps be understood from the individualist perspective: an attempt to constrain the rights of individuals in the greater collective interest is unacceptable, even if this leaves some people without health insurance. Rationing by need is seen as unacceptably interventionist for all but the very poorest. The understanding of equal rights in the US emphasises equality of freedom and does not aim for equality of outcome. This stands in marked contrast to the social solidarity egalitarianism of Sweden.

Need and ability to benefit: the UK's utilitarian approach to equality

By contrast with the US, the UK National Health Service was designed to eliminate ability to pay as the main determinant of access to health care, and adopted the principle of equal access for equal need – even if in practice it frequently falls short of the ideal. The National Health Service Act 1946 established

> a comprehensive health service designed to secure improvement in the physical and mental health of the people of England and Wales . . . The services so provided shall be free of charge.

The aims of the Act are crucial in understanding the attitude of successive governments to rationing. Although it quickly became apparent that the NHS could not meet all demands, and charges were introduced to help control expenditure, the principle of a comprehensive service free to all citizens has a powerful hold over politicians and public. Any attempt by government to exclude elements of health care from the NHS is seen as a threat to this principle, and is therefore a risky electoral strategy. Rationing has therefore generally been implicit.

In some ways, the egalitarian and communitarian ideals of the NHS are an anomaly in a society which otherwise favours individualism and self-reliance. Even Beveridge, who proposed the foundation of the NHS, endorsed an unequal distribution of resources and said the state should not

> stifle incentive, opportunity, responsibility; in establishing a minimum, it should leave room and encouragement for voluntary action by each individual to provide more than that minimum for himself and his family.[14]

The NHS has survived a climate of reducing the welfare state and reverting to privatisation, and has maintained its largely utilitarian approach of maximising the health of the nation. However, this utilitarianism has never been particularly overt. Although trade-offs are made implicitly all the time between the needs of one individual and another, and between the needs of individuals and the interests of the population as a whole, the public perception has been that by and large the NHS meets most individual needs. Acceptance that the NHS cannot afford everything has not been translated directly into acceptance of rationing, a term which for many suggests extreme scarcity and national crisis. Waiting lists have been tolerated as fair turns for everybody, holding out the prospect that one's needs will be met eventually.

More recently, the accumulation of financial pressures on the NHS as part of the general reduction in the welfare state has made it increasingly difficult to hold the implicit rationing line. Managers and clinicians have felt compelled to pursue more explicit and radical approaches. One view that has been gaining ground is that the twin (utilitarian) concepts of health gain and ability to benefit should be the main criteria for decision-making. Supporters of explicit rationing often argue it is the best way to ensure services are targeted at those who can benefit most, thereby maximising health gain for the community as a whole and ensuring the most equitable allocation of resources possible.[15]

However, this exposes the utilitarian premise of the NHS more clearly than ever before. The public becomes uncomfortably aware of rationing decisions, and fears that individual rights to treatment are under threat. These fears have been reinforced by a number of high profile cases where high cost treatments have been denied even though some individuals might benefit. The suggestion that the NHS is there to maximise benefit seems at odds with the public perception of it as the embodiment of solidarity and equality, founded on altruistic care for individuals. The difficulty we all face in acknowledging these hard choices so explicitly has been examined by Coast.[16]

Klein et al. identify a trend away from explicit rationing by exclusion, towards a reconciliation between explicit and implicit approaches.[17] Whilst health gain and ability to benefit continue to inform the development of explicit guidelines and criteria for priority-setting at a population level, the approach recognises the continuing need for interpretation of these by individual clinicians for individual patients. This is undoubtedly partly an appropriate response to the complex realities of clinical decision-making. However, perhaps it is also an indirect response to public reaction to recent explicit rationing decisions. Stark demonstration that individual needs may not be met has threatened to undermine social solidarity in support of the NHS. Political refusal publicly to countenance rationing may protect society from potentially greater inequities;[18] it may also, by offering the public refuge from hard choices, improve the chances of maintaining public confidence in and support for the NHS.

Universal health care in a market liberal environment: the case of New Zealand

The election of the right-wing National Party to power in New Zealand in 1990 heralded a period of economic restraint and reduction of the welfare state. As Ashton notes, 'the ideology underpinning these policies includes a general belief in the superiority of markets over governments, of competition over co-operation and of self-reliance over community responsibility.'[19] Boston and Dalziel discuss the abandonment of any commitment to an egalitarian society by the New Zealand government and note that 'important values such as human dignity, distributive justice, and social cohesion, have been given second place to the pursuit of efficiency, self-reliance, a fiscal balance, and a more limited state.'[20]

In line with this broader movement, New Zealand's tax-funded National Health Service was restructured in 1991 with a purchaser/provider split. As in the Netherlands, the government began to explore issues of priority-setting in parallel with the market reforms, led by a national commission. The original intention was to draw up a list of core services to be included in public health coverage. Hunter suggests that, unlike the Netherlands, the motivation was to promote private insurance and restrict public expenditure by excluding services, rather than ensuring the population had protected access to comprehensive basic coverage.[21] The net effect may be the same, but the difference in perspective could reveal crucial differences in underlying values.

In practice the motivation behind the core services initiative is unclear; although it is consistent with the ideological commitment to self-reliance and liberty underpinning other reforms, it can also be seen as an attempt to moderate the effect of market forces through central state intervention, and reassert the claims of universal equality and community. The government's own White Paper says

> in the past, rationing has been done informally and often without public scrutiny or control. Defining a set of 'core health services' more explicitly will help ensure that the services the public believe to be the most important will be provided. It will also acknowledge more honestly that there are limits to the health services we can afford.[22]

This would suggest that the government did see more positive reasons for identifying core services, although of course the reasoning given in public documents does not always reflect underlying political aims. Cooper summarises the ambiguity thus: 'The core, in short, was to be both a statement of entitlement to the electorate and a way of capping the risk to the state.' In fact the risk to the State could increase, as 'rationing by means of a clearly defined core could make pressure for increased expenditure more difficult to resist.'[23]

Whatever the Government's motivation, the Core Services Committee (CSC)[24] itself clearly felt it had a responsibility to the community. It set out four principles for health care decision-making:

What are the benefits?
Is it value for money?
Is it fair?
Is it consistent with the community's values and priorities?[25]

The question 'is it fair?' means 'is it fair to use the money for this person now rather than use it in some other way?' Benefit means the benefit of

> a particular service to a particular person at a particular time . . . It is too inflexible to judge the usefulness of services according to hard and fast rules. Instead, usefulness should be judged in relation to the individual in need. The question is therefore not so much *which* services should be publicly funded, but rather, *whether and when* a service should be publicly funded.[26]

As this suggests, the CSC quickly decided that its original task of establishing a definitive list of core services was impossible and that a list approach 'is overly simplistic and potentially unfair'.[27] The committee has therefore thrown its efforts into the systematic development of guidelines and criteria for assessing which patients should have priority for access to publicly funded services.

One development is the establishment of nationally agreed criteria for access to waiting lists and for prioritising patients once on the list. A scoring system has been introduced for coronary artery by-pass operations, and patients whose score does not reach a certain level will not be booked for an operation. Clinicians have agreed to work with this threshold, although they regard it as too high, and believe it excludes many people they think would benefit from treatment.[28] This approach explicitly acknowledges both the clinical ideal of individual treatment and the social reality of limited funding, and seeks to make a consistent and equitable trade-off between them.

Although clinical effectiveness provides one of the main criteria for decision-making, low priority for society as a whole comes into play in determining access to services such as cosmetic surgery. The CSC also encourages debate on the use of social criteria such as employment status, responsibility for dependants, marital status, unwillingness to stop smoking or lose weight, age and ability to enjoy leisure activities.[29]

The direction in which the CSC has evolved reaffirms the importance of equal access for equal need, with a utilitarian emphasis on effectiveness and ability to benefit. Autonomy and individual rights are not allowed to override the collective interests of the community; indeed, 'the community's values and priorities' are given an explicit place in the decision-making process. Recent moves to reduce health service competition and restore central planning and regulation under the new coalition government also seem to reaffirm New Zealand's commitment to a universal, national health service.

'Communitarian Illusions'[30]: can the Netherlands reconcile solidarity with autonomy?

As in New Zealand, the Dutch approach to explicit rationing is connected with the structural reforms of the government-commissioned Dekker Report.[31]

One aim of the Dekker Report was to introduce competition between the sick funds (the basis of the Dutch social insurance system) and between them and private insurers. The sick funds are an important legacy of community organisation in the Netherlands, which Therborn describes as 'pillarisation': a system of closed, parallel and hierarchical organisations, held together by a common cultural orientation, including religious groups and unions.[32] Dutch welfare therefore includes public funding of private and religious charities, including hospitals. Therborn suggests pillarisation tends to prefer self-reliance and family responsibility over state intervention, but also promotes a more generous, charitable approach to assisting the poor than the minimum safety-net of many market liberal countries.

One feature of the sick fund system was that different socio-economic and occupational groups had access to different levels of benefit entitlement. A key proposal of the Dekker Report was to remove this differentiation and give everyone mandatory insurance rights. The report of the Dunning Committee was intended to advise on which aspects of health services should form part of these mandatory social insurance arrangements.[33] The spirit of its enquiry was to make sure people were included in coverage, given a fixed budget, rather than deliberately to exclude.

In this cost-limited context the Dunning Committee sought to establish a package of 'basic health care for all'.[34] In examining what constitutes necessary care, it identifies three perspectives from which the need for health care can be defined: the *individual* approach (based on patient self-determination and autonomy), the *medical-professional* approach (in which health is the absence of disease and effectiveness is defined in purely medical terms) and the *community-oriented* approach (which defines health as the ability to function normally in society and gives priority to care which is essential for the community as a whole).

At the macro-level of making choices, 'the Committee prefers a community-oriented approach in which individual rights and professional autonomy are limited in the interests of equity and solidarity',[35] although they continue to have a role at lower levels of decision-making within the constraints imposed at macro-level. To put this into practice, the committee identifies four criteria or 'sieves' which should be applied before any existing types of care are included within the basic package:

1 Is it necessary care, from the community point of view?
2 Is it demonstrated to be effective?

3 Is it efficient?
4 Can it be left to individual responsibility?

On the strength of the Dunning Report, some marginal services have already been excluded, including homeopathy, adult dental care and unevaluated new technologies. However, van de Ven reports that

> the Committee has applied its criteria to several forms of health services and concluded that it is not a simple matter, on the basis of these criteria, to leave complete services or parts of them out of the basic benefits package. The major reason for this is that effectiveness of care has to be considered in relation to the medical indication and the condition of the patient.[36]

The upshot of this is that the committee has not in fact come up with a clearly defined basic package. Instead, it has used its four criteria to develop and apply guidelines to determine which patients should have access to care and under what circumstances they should receive it. The parallels with New Zealand are striking.

A number of writers have commented on the ethical issues underlying the Dutch approach to priority-setting. Ten Have and Keasberry argue that it is founded on two equally strongly held principles, solidarity and equity.[37] The proposed social insurance changes suggest that the understanding of community is increasingly moving from the traditional 'pillarised' account to a more egalitarian, 'whole society' version of solidarity. This implies a shift from a reliance on charitable support and mutual self-help towards an emphasis on rights or entitlements, and a stronger role for the state.

Zwart argues that, given this emphasis on individual rights, the Dunning Report is not as communitarian as it may appear.[38] He contrasts it with the more overtly communitarian position of writers such as Callahan, who argues society's definition of a good and fulfilled life must take priority over the individual's freedom to pursue treatment. Callahan proposes, for example, a universal age-limit for all life-extending treatment.[39] The Dunning Report, Zwart suggests, does not go so far in ranking the community above the individual, and displays some of the values of liberalism.

Van Willigenburg, however, feels the committee has 'walked into a trap which philosophers like Daniel Callahan have been setting during recent years'.[40] He is pessimistic about the chances of arriving at workable priority-setting criteria if 'necessary care' is defined from the community-oriented perspective as care which 'enables an individual to share, maintain and if possible to improve his/her life together with other members of the community'.[41] In trying to develop a definition which 'transcends individual preferences but which may still be acceptable to different individuals' the committee comes up with something 'too vague to have the necessary steering power to exclude unnecessary healthcare'. Any attempt at macro-level to determine what interferes with normal social functioning without reference to 'the unique situation of the individual patient' is bound to fail; it is a 'communitarian illusion'.[42]

Actual choices about resource allocation are made at 'shop-floor' level between doctors and patients; the only way to get 'reasonable control over these processes of day-to-day healthcare allocation is to try to understand the history, laws, habits and contingencies of these processes'.[43] This does not mean accepting a simple model of individual and professional rights and autonomy in place of com-munitarianism, but rather a relational approach. This entails mutual determination of what care is necessary through dialogue between 'critical doctors and well-informed patients'. This may be set within a loose framework of discussion by society about the limits of necessary care, but the macro-level lacks powerful enough criteria to achieve cost-containment.

The Dutch experience thus exemplifies the difficulties in trying to find an acceptable balance between society's need to control expenditure and individuals' need for health care. Attempting to equate individual interests with the community's interests fails to acknowledge the fundamental tensions which may exist between them, with potentially damaging consequences for the maintenance of social cohesion. In the meantime, the financial problems remain unsolved.

Conclusion

The cases described above serve to illustrate a number of issues:

- the diversity of understanding between nations of what consti-tutes an equitable distribution of healthcare resources;
- the difficulty within nations of reconciling competing values, and of defining them;

- the fact that health care sometimes challenges or contradicts otherwise prevailing views of equity;
- the problems of translating principles into acceptable practice.

The process of finding an acceptable balance between different moral principles is perhaps something each country has to go through for itself. We may have to accept Maclean's view that 'there is no unique set of moral principles'; there can be rational answers to moral questions, but not 'a uniquely rational answer . . . There is *more than one thing* it is rational to think.'[44]

In several countries there is evidence of a 'realisation that the idea of devising a simple set of rules is flawed'[45] and disillusion with the view that it is possible to find a way of ordering principles that will enable rational decision-making in practice. This phase is leading in two complementary directions. First, the focus is shifting towards the openness and accountability of the *process* by which decisions are made, in the hope that this will make the decisions defensible even if not everybody agrees with them. Second, there is growing emphasis on clinical guidelines as a way to manage complexity – one example, perhaps, of a procedural framework, within which decisions for individuals can be taken flexibly.

This is not to say, however, that all decisions are equally valid or right. We may indeed be able to establish that some extreme versions of the trade-off between liberty, equality and social solidarity will not meet the claims of justice.

> A well-functioning society recognises the needs of the individual, the needs of society and the interdependence of each with the other . . . Libertarian societies (and so stark capitalism), by giving pre-eminence to individuals and by denying beneficent obligations, defeat any meaningful solidarity and produce societies in which many will lead impoverished lives. Starkly communitarian societies . . . by denigrating individuals merely to servants of the community, likewise defeat meaningful solidarity and result in impoverished lives. Neither can long endure.[46]

Notes

This chapter draws on C. Ham and L. Locock, *International Approaches to Priority Setting in Health Care*, Birmingham: Health Services Management Centre, Handbook Series 25, 1998, published with the support of the Gatsby Foundation.

I should like to thank Dr Roger Crisp, Fellow and Tutor in Philosophy at St Anne's College, Oxford, for helpful comments on an earlier draft, and Susan Law for advice and suggestions. Neither is responsible for any remaining weaknesses.

1 I. Berlin, *Four Essays on Liberty*, Oxford: Oxford University Press, 1969.
2 J. S. Mill, *Utilitarianism*, London, 1863, ch. 5.
3 Working Group on Prioritisation in Healthcare, *From Values to Choices: Report of the Working Group on Prioritisation in Healthcare (Arvoista valintoihin Sosiaala-ja terveydenhuollon priorisointiryhmän raportti)*, Helsinki: National Research and Development Centre for Welfare and Health (STAKES), 1995, p. 44.
4 Swedish Healthcare and Medical Priorities Commission, *No Easy Choices: The Difficult Priorities of Healthcare (Vårdens svåra val)*, Stockholm: Ministry of Health and Social Affairs, SOU, 1993: 93, p. 15.
5 Swedish Parliamentary Priorities Commission, *Priorities in Healthcare: Ethics, Economy, Implementation (Vårdens svåra val: slutbetänkande av Prioriteringsutredningen)*, Stockholm: Ministry of Health and Social Affairs, SOU 1995: 5.
6 Swedish Healthcare and Medical Priorities Commission, *No Easy Choices*, p. 12.
7 Swedish Parliamentary Priorities Commission, *Priorities in Healthcare*.
8 J. Calltorp, 'Sweden: No Easy Choices', in R. Maxwell (ed.) *Rationing Healthcare*, British Medical Bulletin 51 no. 4, Edinburgh: Churchill Livingstone, 1995.
9 S. Holm, 'Goodbye to the Simple Solutions: the Second Phase of Priority Setting in Health Care', *British Medical Journal* 317 (1998), 1000–2, see p. 1000.
10 Oregon Health Services Commission, *Prioritization of Health Services: A Report to the Governor and Legislature*, Salem: Oregon Health Services Commission, 1991, p. 1 of overview.
11 R. Klein, 'On the Oregon Trail: Rationing Healthcare', *British Medical Journal* 302 (1991), pp. 1–2.
12 F. Honigsbaum, 'Who Shall Live? Who Shall Die? Oregon's Health Financing Proposals', London: King's Fund College, 1991, p. 42.
13 D. Callahan, 'Ethics and Priority Setting in Oregon', *Health Affairs* 10 (1991), pp. 78–87. A. Etzioni, 'Healthcare Rationing: A Critical Evaluation', *Health Affairs* 10 (1991), pp. 88–95.
14 Lord W. Beveridge, *Voluntary Action*, London: Allen and Unwin, 1948.
15 A. Maynard, 'Rationing Healthcare', *British Medical Journal* 313 (1996), p. 1499.
16 J. Coast, 'Rationing within the NHS should be explicit – the case against', *British Medical Journal* 314 (1997), pp. 1118–22.

17 R. Klein, P. Day and S. Redmayne, *Managing Scarcity*, Buckingham: Open University Press, 1996.
18 D. Hunter, *Rationing Dilemmas in Health Care*, Birmingham: National Association of Health Authorities and Trusts (NAHAT), 1993.
19 T. Ashton, 'From Evolution to Revolution: Restructuring the New Zealand Health System', in D. Seedhouse (ed.) *Reforming Healthcare: The Philosophy and Practice of International Healthcare Reform*, Chichester: Wiley, 1995, p. 88.
20 J. Boston and P. Dalziel, *The Decent Society*, Oxford: Oxford University Press, 1992.
21 H. Hunter, 'New Zealand Chops', *Health Service Journal*, 9 May 1996, pp. 20–3.
22 New Zealand Minister of Health, *Your Health and the Public Health (Green and White Paper): A Statement of Government Health Policy*, Wellington: Minister of Health, 1991, p. 80.
23 M. H. Cooper, 'Core Services and the New Zealand Health Reforms', in R. Maxwell (ed.) *Rationing Healthcare*, British Medical Bulletin, vol. 51, no. 4, Edinburgh: Churchill Livingstone, 1995, p. 804.
24 Commonly used name for the National Advisory Committee.
25 National Advisory Committee on Health and Disability Support Services, *The Best of Health 2: How We Decide on the Health and Disability Support Services We Value Most*, Wellington: National Advisory Committee on Core Health and Disability Support Services, 1993.
26 Ibid., p. 17.
27 National Advisory Committee on Health and Disability Support Services, *Core Services 1994/95*, Wellington: National Advisory Committee on Core Health and Disability Support Services, 1993, p. 17.
28 D. Hadorn and A. Holmes, 'The New Zealand Priority Criteria Project. Part I: Overview, Part II: Coronary Artery Bypass Graft Surgery', *British Medical Journal* 314 (1997), pp. 131–8.
29 National Advisory Committee on Core Health and Disability Support Services, *Core Services for 1995/96*, Wellington: National Advisory Committee on Core Health and Disability Support Services, 1994.
30 T. van Willigenburg, 'Communitarian Illusions: Or Why the Dutch Proposal for Setting Priorities in Health Care Must Fail', in D. Seedhouse (ed.) *Reforming Healthcare: The Philosophy and Practice of International Healthcare Reform*, Chichester: Wiley, 1995.
31 Commissie Structuur en Financiering Gezondheidszorg, *Bereidheid tot Verandering*, The Hague: DOP, 1987.
32 G. Therborn, 'Pillarisation and Popular Movements', in F. Castles (ed.) *The Comparative History of Public Policy*, Cambridge: Polity Press, 1989.
33 Government Committee on Choices in Healthcare, *Choices in Healthcare*, Rijswijk, Minsitry of Welfare, Health and Cultural Affairs, 1992.
34 Ibid., p. 14.
35 Ibid., p. 23.
36 W. P. M. M. van de Ven, 'Choices in Healthcare: A Contribution from the Netherlands', in R. Maxwell (ed.) *Rationing Healthcare*, British Medical Bulletin, vol. 51, no. 4, Edinburgh: Churchill Livingstone, 1995, p. 789.

37 H. Ten Have and H. Keasberry, 'Equity and Solidarity: The Context of Healthcare in The Netherlands', *Journal of Medicine and Philosophy* 17(4) (1992), 463–77.
38 H. Zwart, 'Rationing in the Netherlands: The Liberal and the Communitarian Perspective', *Healthcare Analysis* 1(1) (1993), pp. 53–6.
39 D. Callahan, *Setting Limits: Medical Goals in an Ageing Society*, New York: Simon and Schuster, 1987.
40 T. van Willigenburg, 'Communitarian Illusions', p. 163.
41 Government Committee on Choices in Health Care, *Choices in Healthcare*.
42 T. van Willigenburg, 'Communitarian Illusions', pp. 163–4.
43 Ibid., p. 164.
44 A. Maclean, *The Elimination of Morality: Reflections on Utilitarianism and Bioethics*, London: Routledge, 1993.
45 S. Holm, 'Goodbye to the Simple Solutions', p. 1000.
46 E. Loewy, 'Of Markets, Technology, Patients and Profits', in D. Seedhouse (ed.) *Reforming Healthcare: The Philosophy and Practice of International Healthcare Reform*, Chichester: Wiley, 1995.

Part II

SCREENING

In this section of the book, the issues concerning screening for ill health are considered. Screening is a fundamental tool for disease prevention and health promotion and is therefore a major weapon for public health.

In the first chapter Troop discusses when screening programmes can be justified. It is obviously important that screening programmes do more good than harm. In view of recent 'scares' about screening programmes, she describes the importance of having quality assurance mechanisms and of clearly communicating the purpose and limits of screening programmes to the public. Solbakk and Hasan consider the case of genetic screening in the context of prioritisation and the problems of communicating ideas about risk. In the absence of evidence to show overall health benefit for the population, the case for funding genetic screening programmes seems poor. Camilleri-Ferrante considers antenatal screening and concentrates on screening for diseases that may lead to the abortion of a foetus. This issue is inevitably complex, and arguments about the status of the foetus are outlined. Stewart-Brown considers childhood screening programmes, which she argues are mostly of unproven benefit to the population. She suggests that professionals should tell parents about the level of evidence for the benefits of screening programmes, so that they can choose whether to attend.

In conclusion, the term 'screening' is used for a wide range of health programmes, most of which do not meet the quality criteria outlined in the first chapter of this section. In this respect, many screening programmes could be criticised. These chapters offer a snapshot of the complex ethical issues encountered by such programmes.

6

SCREENING: GENERAL PRINCIPLES

Pat Troop

Screening can be defined as

> The systematic application of a test or enquiry, to identify
> individuals at sufficient risk of a specific disorder to warrant
> further investigation or direct preventive action, amongst
> persons who have not sought medical attention on account
> of symptoms of that disorder.[1]

All forms of health care raise ethical issues, many of which apply to
screening. However, screening has important differences from other
types of health care. In most situations, the patient approaches the
clinician, who will then offer treatment on the basis of current evidence of what is most effective. In some cases, even if the evidence
is limited, the clinician may still offer whatever treatment appears
best rather than not treat the patient at all. In screening, the
health service or health professionals are saying to apparently
healthy people, 'Come to us, go through this procedure, and there
will be a benefit'. Under those circumstances, it is imperative that
there is evidence of benefit, and that the collective benefits will outweigh the side-effects or the harm from the screening programme.

There have been criteria for assessing screening for many years.
Wilson and Junger published *The Principles and Practice of Screening for Disease* in 1968.[2] The principles have broadly stood the test
of time, although the UK National Screening Committee have
recently revised them,[3] to take into account the increasing recognition that screening programmes can have harmful side-effects as
well as benefits (see Table 6.1). It is the proactive nature of screening,

Table 6.1 Criteria for assessing screening

The condition
 1 The condition should be an important health problem.
 2 (i)   The epidemiology of the condition should be known.
   (ii) The natural history of the condition should be understood.
   (iii) There should be a recognised latent period or early symptomatic stage.
 3 All the cost-effective primary prevention interventions should have been implemented as far as practicable.

The test
 4 There should be a simple, safe, precise and validated screening test.
 5 The distribution of test values in the target population should be known and a suitable cut-off level defined and agreed.
 6 The test should be acceptable to the population.
 7 There should be an agreed policy on the further diagnostic investigation of individuals with a positive test result and on the choices available to those individuals.

The treatment
 8 There should be an effective treatment or intervention for patients identified through early detection.
 9 There should be agreed evidence-based policies covering which individuals should be offered treatment and the appropriate treatment to be offered.
10 Clinical management of the condition and patient outcomes should be optimised by all health care providers prior to participation in a screening programme.

The screening programme
11 There should be evidence from high quality Randomised Controlled Trials that the screening programme is effective in reducing mortality or morbidity.
12 There should be evidence that the complete screening programme (test, diagnostic procedures, treatment/intervention) is clinically, socially and ethically acceptable to health professionals and the public.
13 The benefit from the screening programme should outweigh the physical and psychological harm (caused by the test, diagnostic procedures and treatment).
14 The opportunity cost of the screening programme (including testing, diagnosis and treatment) should be economically balanced in relation to expenditure on medical care as a whole.
15 There should be a plan for managing and monitoring the screening programme and an agreed set of quality assurance standards.
16 Adequate staffing and facilities for testing, diagnosis, treatment and programme management should be available prior to the commencement of the screening programme.
17 All other options for managing the condition should have been considered (e.g. improving treatment, providing other services).

Source: First Report of the National Screening Committee, Health Departments of the United Kingdom, April 1998.

along with this need to balance benefit and harm, that raises particular ethical issues.

The context for screening

Even with the revised criteria for assessing screening, the decision whether or not to screen should not be taken in isolation, but in the overall context of the health problem to be tackled and the potential for other approaches. Screening is an example of secondary prevention, that is, early identification of a problem to prevent or reduce its effect. In some situations, primary prevention, which is aimed at preventing the disease arising, may be an option. For example, pilot programmes to assess the potential for screening for colorectal cancer are to be introduced in the UK,[4] but these also need to be compared with the potential benefit from dietary change, as there is evidence that diet can influence the development of colorectal cancer.[5] However, primary prevention is difficult to assess. It is not enough to recognise the link between diet and cancer. To compare the benefits with screening, we need to know the size of the benefit and the time-scale for demonstrating it, as well as the effectiveness of the different approaches to bring about the change in diet. Lifestyle changes are notoriously difficult to evaluate. They do not lend themselves easily to the clinical trial model, as there are many influences on lifestyle that are difficult to control. As behaviour is affected by a wide range of influences, the other factors may also affect the effectiveness of the intervention. Therefore, screening may be seen as the easier, albeit costly, option, as its potential can be more easily demonstrated.

The pressure to introduce screening is understandable. It seems to fit the maxim 'prevention is better than cure'. This may be true in some cases, but in others it may be an illusion, for example, because of the concept of lag time. This is illustrated in Figure 6.1.

After diagnosis the average survival time from a disease may be 10 years. After screening has been introduced for that disease the average survival time following diagnosis through screening becomes 15 years. This appears to improve the survival time by 5 years. However, it may just be that screening advances the diagnosis by an average of 5 years. The disease is picked up at an earlier stage, but the overall outcome in terms of survival is not improved. Screening is only successful if the earlier identification leads to more effective treatment which delays mortality. Without knowing the

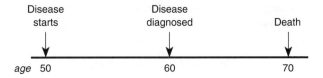

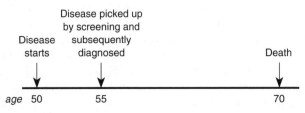

Figure 6.1 Lag time

time from the start of the disease to diagnosis, such assessments can only be made using long-term follow-up studies.

The push for more screening

The general belief that 'prevention is better than cure' often results from pressure from interested groups and the media. For example in the UK, there has been pressure to introduce screening for prostate cancer. For many people there is a natural belief that early detection should lead to early treatment and therefore better outcome. However, two reports commissioned through the Health Technology Assessment programme,[6] concluded that, whilst there was the technology for screening, a benefit in the form of reduced mortality had not been demonstrated. On the other hand, the treatment that would follow a positive result could have worrying side-effects and thus do more harm than good. Therefore, despite the evidence that early detection was possible, the National Screening Committee recommended that screening should not be introduced.

The introduction of new technology is often another driver for introducing screening. Once it is possible to test for a condition and the technology becomes widely available, there is often pressure to introduce routine testing or screening. Neonatal screening for phenylketonuria and hypothyroidism is well established, and the technology now exists to broaden the range of tests that can be applied to the same blood sample.[7] The evidence of benefit is lacking, but once technology is available, it is often difficult to prevent the spread of testing.

The aims of screening

When screening is considered the most appropriate response to a health problem, the aims of the programme need to be defined. There may be a conflict between the aims of those planning the programme and those using the programme. For example, programmes are usually planned on a population basis. They are assessed in such terms as the detection rate, the numbers of false positives and false negatives (defined below) and the overall population benefit. No screening test is perfect, and there is always a trade-off, so the planners agree an 'acceptable' level of false results. On the other hand, the individual wishes to know the answer to 'Do I have the disease or not, and what is the benefit to me?'

The uncertainties of screening are often not recognised by the general public, therefore errors which fall within the acceptable range for the planners may be seen as failures in the screening programme by the public. This has been demonstrated in the cervical screening programme. There have been genuine failures in the delivery of the programme that have undermined public confidence. However, in any programme that has a quality assurance system and where there is routine monitoring against standards, results will sometimes be found which are outside or at the limit of the 'acceptable' range, and action will be needed to redress the situation. This has been the situation in some of the 'recall' episodes. These can be regarded as failures of the screening, or successes of the quality assurance scheme. The higher the standards are set, the more likely are 'failures' to be identified.

The expected outcomes for programmes need to be explicit. These could be in terms of the benefit to the population as a whole, such as to reduce the prevalence of condition in the community, or to reduce the overall mortality. They could also be defined in terms of the rights of individuals. For example, the programme could enable them to make informed decisions about their own health, such as about changing their lifestyle or accepting treatment. Individuals using the programme will assume that each one of them might benefit from screening whereas in reality many programmes are planned on the basis of the net benefit to the population.

How the aims of the programme are defined will affect how the programme is offered, and how its success is measured. For example, the breast screening programme was planned on a population basis. The level of uptake of screening is important for achieving the population benefit from the programme, and hence is monitored and measured as a standard and success factor. However, it could be argued that the purpose of screening for Down's Syndrome is to enable women to make informed choices about their pregnancies. Therefore, measuring the success of the programme in population terms would be inappropriate. It would be more appropriate to monitor the number of women offered the test and able to make an informed choice.

Understanding the disease

One of the criteria for assessing screening programmes is that the natural history of the disease should be known. The concept of 'lag time' has already been referred to. Those identified through screening may not have improved outcomes, but they would be aware of their diagnosis for longer, which could cause anxiety. On the other hand, the treatment needed may be less invasive at that stage, so that overall morbidity may be reduced. In some situations, the progression of the disease may not be uniform. For example, in cervical screening, early changes may regress and not progress to cancer. If this is not recognised and early changes treated, some individuals may be subjected to unnecessary treatment. Long-term studies are needed to determine these sorts of factors, which may be difficult to balance against the pressure to introduce screening.

Some screening detects risk factors for a disease. Knowing the potential for having the disease can confer benefit, because the individual can choose to take preventive action. On the other hand, it could create anxiety without improving the health of the individual. Through the study of genetics, it is being recognised that for certain risk factors there are susceptible individuals within a population. Therefore, some people with the risk factors may not progress to the disease. It may become more difficult to justify total population screening, when only a minority are likely to benefit.

The limits of testing

Few tests are 100 per cent accurate. There are some blood tests, for example for hepatitis B or syphilis, which are based on the presence or otherwise of antibodies, and which therefore do have a high level of accuracy. Others, such as cervical and breast screening rely on human judgement to detect changes. For some conditions, such as serum testing for the risk of Down's Syndrome, there are continuous variables. A cut-off point for deciding which women should be

Table 6.2 The outcomes of screening

	Disease present	Disease absent	
Test positive	true positive A	false positive B	A + B
Test negative	false negative C	true negative D	C + D
	A + C	B + D	

sensitivity	= the proportion of people with the disease in whom the finding is positive = A/(A + C)
specificity	= the proportion of people without the disease in whom the finding is negative = D/(B + D)

offered the diagnostic test has to be agreed. Therefore there are a number of outcomes of screening. (See Table 6.2.)

The ideal test is 100 per cent sensitive and 100 per cent specific, but this is rarely, if ever, achieved. There are always those who have the condition who are missed (false negatives), and those who do not have the condition who are falsely identified as positive (false positives). Most systems have procedures to minimise false negatives, such as rapid re-screening in cervical screening. Nevertheless, cases are missed, and there is concern that those people may disregard symptoms in the belief that screening has declared them free from disease. Screening tests are not diagnostic, and therefore, those among the positive who are false positive should be identified at the follow-up diagnostic procedure. Nevertheless, positive results can create anxiety, and this is not always alleviated when the diagnostic test confirms the absence of disease. In one study,[8] more women who had had a false positive mammogram were affected by worry three months later than women who had had a normal mammogram.

As already indicated, many screening tests are not based on yes or no answers. They may be based on continual variables or a combination of factors, such as a woman's age and serum testing for Down's Syndrome. They suggest the probability of the presence of Down's Syndrome and in these situations there is always a trade-off between sensitivity and specificity. Serra-Prat and his colleagues

assessed this trade-off for different combinations of screening procedures for Down's Syndrome, and using different cut-off points
for the test.[9] The approach that achieved the highest detection
rate rewarded sensitivity over specificity. Therefore a high detection
rate was associated with a high false positive rate, and hence a high
rate of diagnostic tests. For Down's Syndrome, this usually involves
amniocentesis, which carries a risk of about 1 per cent foetal loss.
Those programmes that aimed to minimise foetal loss were associated with a lower detection rate. Where should the balance lie?
Should the aim be to identify as many affected pregnancies as possible, to enable women to make informed choices, but with a risk
of a high rate of foetal loss, or should it be to minimise foetal loss,
leaving a greater number of women with affected pregnancies not
able to make those choices? Such decisions are value judgements,
which raises the question of whose values should be paramount,
the individuals' or professionals'. In the UK National Screening
Committee, there are consumer representatives, but programmes
are still planned to be offered in a standard way by professionals.
Serra-Prat and his colleagues suggest an alternative would be to
explain to women the pros and cons of different screening
approaches, and allow them to make a choice based on their own
values.

This balance of benefit and harm is also demonstrated in breast
screening. These have been assessed by Sox,[10] who put forward
figures from a number of studies to show that for women aged
50–79 years, the reduction in mortality from breast cancer was
26 per cent, and the gap in mortality between those screened and
controls became apparent after four years. The cumulative false
positive rate after ten mammograms was 47.3 per cent. He argued
that most women would accept that trade-off. However for
women aged 40–9, the difference in mortality was 16 per cent, and
the benefit did not become apparent until after tren years. For this
age group the cumulative false positive mammogram rate was
56.2 per cent. Therefore, whilst the case for screening older women
may be reasonable, it is less convincing for younger women. In a
similar way to Serra-Prat and his colleagues, Sox argues that the
role of the physician is to advise women of all the information
that would enable her to make a decision based on her own values.

Whilst the major problems are associated with false positives and
false negatives, and the balance between them, there can also be
problems with true negatives and true positives. Breast screening
only identifies disease at the time of screening, so women who have

negative results need to be informed that new cancers can still arise, and they should still come forward with symptoms, and return for re-screening at regular intervals.

Some conditions, such as HIV, can carry stigma, and this can result in problems with employment and insurance. Therefore for pregnant women, when the benefits of treatment were not clear, the balance of benefit and harm seemed tipped towards not screening, and the policy in the UK has been to offer women voluntary testing, particularly in areas of high prevalence. Treatment now offers real benefits for mother and child. Therefore the balance may have changed. In the USA, routine testing is recommended for all pregnant women, and the annual numbers of births of infected children have declined.[11] Despite the guidance on offering testing in the UK, the number of tests offered and the uptake varies from hospital to hospital, and the same decline in the number of affected births has not been seen in the UK.

This also raises the question, is routine testing the same as screening? It is UK policy to offer all women testing for hepatitis B, and this is called screening. If routine testing for HIV is offered to all women, then should it be recognised that this is also screening? There are concerns that this might result in a situation where women were tested for HIV along with a range of other tests in the screening programme. They may not therefore make the same active choice, in which they assess both the disadvantages as well as the benefits of screening. On the other hand, there should always be the opportunity for an individual to opt out of any screening programme. This already happens: not all women attend for cervical screening when invited, and some women refuse screening for Down's Syndrome. The advantages of recognising routine testing as screening are that it enables uniform standards and quality assurance processes to be established, which themselves should bring safeguards. However it does assume that all those who attend for screening are fully informed and able to choose.

Delivering the programme

Screening programmes are more than testing. They are complex processes that involve a range of professionals and organisations. The cervical screening programme involves health authorities, primary care teams and a number of different hospital departments. With such a complex system, failures can result at any stage, resulting in major problems.[12] At the beginning of this chapter, the importance of recognising the proactive nature of screening was highlighted, and the need to be able to demonstrate benefit. It is equally important to organise and manage screening so that the benefit is realised and maintained. If it is unethical to offer screening where the benefit is not apparent, it is also unethical to invite people into a screening programme where that benefit is not being realised. Quality assurance mechanisms are essential; the importance of explaining these has already been mentioned.

Those involved in the programme need to be trained appropriately and to be able to explain the principles underlying the test. If those coming forward are to be able to decide whether to opt in or out of the programme, to understand the advantages and disadvantages and to make informed choices, they need information. They do not always receive this, and many health professionals are not able to give accurate information.[13]

The aims of the programme need to be understood by all those involved. If the aim of the programme is to enable people to make choices, those choices must be respected. There is a concern that once someone enters the system, it is assumed they will go right through the system. However, making a decision before testing against a hypothetical situation of a positive test is not the same as making that decision when faced with an actual positive test. It must be possible for an individual to choose to stop at any point in the process.

Nevertheless, it is assumed that the majority of people will want the treatment offered after screening. Programmes are very expensive, and in the UK are paid for by the NHS, which is funded through taxation. If only a small number chooses to go through the screening, or only a small percentage of those who have been screened choose to go on to treatment, could a publicly funded NHS justify the continuation of the programme? This goes back to the different aims of programmes as described earlier. If the aim is to reduce the prevalence of a condition or reduce mortality within a given population, a low uptake of screening or treatment might be grounds for not offering the programme, providing it could be shown that the screening had been offered appropriately and the lack of uptake was as a result of genuine choice. If on the other hand the aim is to offer choice, should the programme be funded if most people choose not to take up treatment and the prevalence of the condition remains the same? It can be argued that people have the right to know about their own health if that information is available, even if they choose not to act on that information. However, in publicly funded services knowledge alone may not be a sufficient benefit compared with the costs of the programme. Therefore, although we may pose the population and individual approaches as quite different, in practice the distinction is not so clear. A programme is unlikely to be offered unless there is a general consensus amongst the population that the prevalence of a condition needs to be reduced or the outcome needs to be improved, such that, when screened, they make the decision to accept treatment.

Conclusion

If we fully understand the natural history of a disease, have a screening test which is 100 per cent accurate, and effective treatment after screening, many of the ethical issues discussed would not be of concern. Some would still remain, such as whether or not it is appropriate to screen for congenital abnormalities, and whether or not universal screening is applicable when only a minority will benefit. But many of the ethical problems currently around screening arise because we do not have a full understanding of the natural history of most diseases, very few tests are 100 per cent accurate, and treatment is often only partially successful or only successful in a proportion of people. Therefore, those planning programmes make judgements about whether it is more important to have a high detection rate at the expense of a high number of false positives, or to minimise the harm from false positives at the expense of detection. They balance the cost of the programme with the gains, and the cost-effectiveness of screening with other approaches. They usually plan the programme on the basis of population benefit, but then offer that programme to people who make decisions on the basis of individual, rather than population, benefit.

If these conflicts are to be reconciled, there needs to be an open discussion about the aims of a programme, and the relative costs and benefits, both to the population and the individual. There needs to be a recognition that many of the decisions are based on value judgements, which suggests that there should be a much wider involvement of those using the programme to bring in different perspectives and values. However, this approach still implies that programmes will be offered in a standard way, albeit having taken into account this wide range of views. On the other hand, no standard programme can respond to the needs of all individuals. In many other aspects of health care, the concept of patient- or client-centred care is now predominant.[14] This raises what appears to be the fundamental ethical issue, that is, who should decide the balance between the benefit and harm. Screening programmes in the UK have been planned on a population basis, and this balance has been decided by those planning the programme. At the moment, the only choice the individual can make is whether to opt in or out of the programme. With the increasing recognition that the individual needs to be at the centre of health care and decision-making about his or her health care, this may not be acceptable. The alternative approaches suggested by some of the authors quoted, which would be to give full information on the alternatives within a screening programme, and to allow the individual to choose may need to be considered.

Notes

1 Fist Report of the National Screening Committee, Health Departments of the United Kingdom, April 1998.
2 Wilson, J. M. G., Junger, G., *The Principles and Practice of Screening for Disease*, Public Health Papers no. 34, Geneva: WHO, 1968, pp. 26–39.
3 First Report of the National Screening Committee.
4 National Screening Committee, 'A proposal for colorectal screening pilots' (forthcoming; personal communication).
5 Working Group on Diet and Cancer of the Committee on Medical Aspects of Food and Nutrition Policy, *Nutritional Aspects of the Development of Cancer*, London: Department of Health, 1998.
6 Chamberlain, J., Melia, J., Moss, S., Brown, J., *The Diagnosis, Management and Costs of Prostate Cancer in England and Wales*, Health Technology Assessment 1997, vol. 1, no. 3. Selley, S., Donovan, J., Faulkner, A., Coast, J., Gillatt, D., *Diagnosis, Management and Screening of Early Localised Prostate Cancer*, Health Technology Assessment 1997, vol .1, no. 2.
7 Seymour, C. A,. Thomason, M. J., Chalmers, R. A., Addison, G. M., Bain, M. D., Cockburn, F., Littlejohns, P., Lord, J., Wilcox, A. H., *Newborn Screening for Inborn Errors of Metabolism: A Systematic Review*, Health Technology Assessment 1997, vol. 1, no. 11.
8 Lerman, C., Trock, B., Rimer, B. K., Boyce, A., Jepson, C., Ensgstrom, P. F., 'Psychological and behavioural implications of abnormal mammograms', *Annals of Internal Medicine* (1991), vol. 114, pp. 657–61.
9 Serra-Prat, M., Gallo, P., Jovell, A. J., Aymerich, M., Estrado, M. D., 'Trade-offs in prenatal detection of Down's syndrome', *American Journal of Public Health* (1998), vol. 88, no. 4, pp. 551–7.
10 Sox, H. C., Editorial, 'Benefit and harm associated with screening for breast cancer', *New England Journal of Medicine* (1998), vol. 338, no. 16, pp. 1145–6.

11 Intercollegiate Working Party for Enhancing Voluntary Confidential HIV Testing in Pregnancy, *Reducing Mother to Child Transmission of HIV Infection in the United Kingdom*, London: Royal College of Paediatrics and Child Health, 1998.
12 Review of Cervical Screening at Kent and Canterbury Hospital NHS Trust, London: Department of Health, 1997.
13 Wald, N. J., Kennard, A., Hackshaw, A., McGuire, A., 'Antenatal screening for Down's syndrome', *Journal of Medical Screening* (1997), vol. 4, pp. 181–246.
14 Expert Maternity Group, *Changing Childbirth*, London: Department of Health, 1993.

7

GENETIC TESTS, SCREENING AND PRIORITIES IN HEALTH CARE

Jan Helge Solbakk and Homa Hasan

Introduction

Man has always been engaged in activities aimed at controlling and fighting threats against life and health. At earlier times magic and religion had important roles to play in explaining disease, death and misfortune, as well as in generating strategies of combat against such dangers. As long as man conceived himself as someone exposed to the shifting tempers of competing deities and nature's powers, disease, death and disasters were received, accepted and experienced as shared evils of humanity.

In a modern society, 'having accepted a purely benevolent God and a devil who has forfeited his cosmological function if not his very existence',[1] we see that this is no longer the case. Today, disease, death and misfortune have become secularised, individualised and privatised. Disease is no longer perceived as a shared common destiny but as an individual experience. Modernity has transformed human destiny into individualised probabilities and misfortunes into privatised forms of risks.

Gradually as man has been successful at controlling nature, an increased awareness of the importance of knowledge and the right decisions to guard against misfortune has emerged. Hence, the need to control these decisions through rational reasoning has grown, and '[r]efusing to assume risks or demanding their rejection have become dangerous behaviour'.[2] We are, so to speak, in the process of entering an era of individualised risk profiles and risk awareness. This is the cultural setting within which predictive medicine tries to find its way as well as its market.

94

In this chapter, genetic testing is defined to be the use of either biochemical or molecular genetic techniques to determine a risk or diagnosis of a specific genetic condition. In our attempt to deal with the problem of priorities in relation to genetic testing and genetic screening, a Socratic approach will be applied. This implies that several 'impertinent' questions will be raised and few answers will be provided.

The purpose of genetic testing and genetic screening

The first Socratic question to raise is the *purpose* of genetic testing and genetic screening; will the information gained be used in prevention or in health care management or in neither? Angus Clarke states that it is paramount to distinguish between different contexts in which genetic testing may be carried out.[3] Of special relevance is the distinction between testing aimed at individuals and population-based screening.

In the instance of *prevention*, there are three modes to consider; primary, secondary and tertiary.[4] *Primary prevention* seeks to remove the cause from a population. For example pre-conceptual folic acid is shown to prevent 75 per cent of neural tube defects from occurring. *Secondary prevention* is aimed at preventing overt clinical cases from presenting. This is achieved by early detection and intervention, as in the cases for screening programs for metabolic diseases in new-borns and screening of adult women for breast cancer or cervical cancer. *Tertiary prevention* is not factually prevention but effective management of a condition, so that the full magnitude of pain and disability associated with the condition are avoided, such as prophylactic mastectomy for 'high' breast cancer risk.

Five clusters of preliminary questions

Before we turn to the most central issue of this chapter, the question of *which* genetic tests and screening programmes should be given priority, five clusters of preliminary questions need to be addressed. First is the *identity of different interest groups* in the field of genetic testing and genetic screening. Who are they? Patients suffering from genetic diseases or extended family members? Patient organisations? Primary care physicians and family physicians? Genetic counsellors? Researchers? Bioethicists? Research companies? Insurance companies? Employers? Employees? The political community? Society?

The second question is *the nature of genetic counselling*. The third is the relationship between *legitimate* and *illegitimate interests* in the field of genetic testing and genetic screening. The fourth is the meaning of self-evident and hidden concepts and values in predictive medicine: what is meant by 'genetic disease', 'serious disease', 'genetic susceptibility', 'to be at risk', 'low risk', 'high risk' and so on? Who has the authority finally to define these concepts, and whose interests are at stake in the process of prescribing this new vocabulary? Last but not least, what are the potential effects and side-effects of genetic testing and screening programmes?

The identity of genetic counsellors and the nature of genetic counselling

It is tempting here to make some further remarks in relation to the most prominent interest groups mentioned above: the genetic counsellors. We tend to believe that we know who they are, but do we really know what characterises their enterprise?

> Are the genetic counsellors perfect, value-neutral experts who have embraced science as a vocation . . . specialists without spirit, sensualists without heart?[5]

Are genetic counsellors likely to be considered as professionals occupied with risk-assessment and non-directive communication of 'necessary facts', enabling their clients to 'make informed independent decisions, free of coercion'?[6]

Although questioning the claim that non-directive practice predominates in clinical genetics, Clarke gives three substantial reasons why 'non-directive counselling' continues to be a precept. First, given the historical context of medical genetics and the terrible consequences of eugenic policies, there is 'the vehemence of the feelings in support of 'non-directiveness', to consider. Second, non-directiveness is in compliance with the leading ethical principle of modern health care, the *respect for autonomy*. Third, 'there is the usefulness for counselors of some [emotional] detachment from the decisions made by their clients'.[7]

Although we are sympathetic to the fact that non-directiveness is considered the golden rule of genetic counselling, we believe that genetic counsellors are more than trained organ grinders dispensing information. Among professionals themselves observations have been made that this ideal is not always achievable in practice, nor is it desirable. This fact makes it all the more interesting to reconsider the practical feasibility of non-directiveness.

Arguments questioning the feasibility of non-directiveness

An argument that questions the feasibility of this ideal relates to the ambiguous concept of risk:

> Understanding the difference between theoretic risks and materialised event makes clear why reproductive decisions are so much more complex than advocates of rational choice models for reproductive behaviour would have it . . . Understanding theoretic risk requires one type of inquiry; understanding materialisation or its opposite, non-occurrence, requires another.[8]

Added to this conceptual problem is '[i]f risks are falsely assessed, the genetic counselling undermines the rational choice and patient autonomy the service was intended to promote'.[9] Clarke draws attention to three further arguments, of which the first seems to undermine non-directiveness in relation to antenatal screening tests:

> While the genetic counseling of individuals and families may often contain no 'directiveness' – it may not be related to decision making at all – there is a clear message conveyed to society at large from the existence of genetic counseling clinics and – a fortiori – from the existence and operation of antenatal genetic screening programs.[10]

His second argument relates to the fact that there is a subpopulation of clients, who want to be actively guided 'as to what course of action to follow'. Thirdly, the fact that 'there are circumstances in which genetic counsellors are expected at least to attempt to persuade their clients to take one course of action rather than another – to share information about the genetic condition in their family with other family members'.[11]

Empirical evidence for several of these arguments is now available in a survey study of American practitioners in the field. Full members of the National Society of Genetic Counselors – 781 of them – were asked to assess how they defined non-directiveness, its importance to their practice, and how and why they were ever directive. Of the 383 respondents almost 96 per cent viewed this

ideal to be important in their practice, but 72 per cent also acknowledged they sometimes acted in a directive way. According to the
authors of this study, '[t]he respondents provided some compelling
reasons for intentionally moving toward more directive responses'.
A problem many practitioners reported was the difficulty in total
avoidance of non-directiveness in the selection of what information
to provide to the clients and what to exclude from them. A second
problem was the impossibility of completely excluding elements of
directiveness embedded in their non-verbal behaviours during the
counselling session. Another important finding was the differentiation made by one of the respondents between directiveness in *process*
versus *directiveness in outcome*. 'This process–outcome distinction is
important', say the authors, since they consider the first mode of
directiveness to comply fully with the 'genetic counselor roles of
expert informant and facilitator'.[12]

As to the question about the acceptability of acting in a directive
way in relation to decision outcomes, the authors take a somewhat
more cautious stand, acknowledging that in *some* situations it may
be appropriate for the genetic counsellor to share what they call
'personal biases' – at least as long as they make it clear to the
client that possessing medical expertise does not furnish them with
any special expertise or competence in matters of values and
moral dilemmas.

The relation between legitimate and illegitimate interests

As already noted it is necessary to evaluate the relation *between
legitimate* and *illegitimate interests* in the field of genetic testing
and genetic screening. *Legitimate interests* can include the well-
being of the patient and his or her family. Obtaining a diagnosis
can be enough to promote parental 'closure', even if there is no effective cure or treatment of the condition. ('Closure' in this context
means a favourable psychological adjustment to the situation.)
For others, it may be the avoidance of a genetic condition either
by prenatal diagnosis or alternative methods of reproduction
(such as sperm- or egg-donation). For some people it is important
to provide as much information as early as possible in order that
they be able to cope with the forthcoming event.

Illegitimate interests can include groups who stand to profit financially by the promotion of the genetic tests and screening programmes they have helped to create. There may be a conflict of

interest when private finance is involved in providing a service, for example, in maintaining absolute neutrality in the face of the temptation to profit. However, patient interests may benefit from private testing being under strict regulation, including auditing the quality of services provided. Methods for advertising should be regulated in order to minimise distress and anxiety in the target populations. In the absence of national policies and guidelines, the very existence of private testing possibilities may create an inequitable service; only those who can afford it will be able to obtain the service.

The relation between self-evident and hidden values

The fourth cluster of questions asks how one can define the concepts used in genetic testing and screening. There are, for example, the concepts of 'disease', 'health', 'normality', 'risk', 'genetic disease' and 'genetic susceptibility'. Many of these definitions are value-laden and yet their definition is central to deciding whether genetic services are useful or justifiable. Today, there seem to be few clear-cut answers to these questions. This is partly due to the fact that they have not yet been raised within the field of medical genetics, and partly, we believe, it is because their answers are considered to be self-evident and therefore unnecessary to deal with. In other words, it seems to be taken for granted that these are questions of a purely scientific nature, and that they fall under the sole purview of scientific practitioners – the experts.

To take an example, the confusing concept of 'genetic disease' conjures the immediate affliction of the condition in question. Often this is a misapprehension, especially in the case of a young person with a late-onset condition. Humans are estimated to have in the region of 100,000 genes. Every individual is thought to have five lethal gene changes, often in non-functional gene sequences. Sometimes these changes occur within gene sequences in a way that may impair the normal gene function. Where the gene function is impaired, the individual is said to have a genetic disorder; where the gene changes do not cause any outward phenotype (compared with 'normal' characteristics) some semblance of genetic order is maintained. On the other hand, it is recognised that being a carrier for some recessive conditions may confer advantages. For example sickle cell trait helps protect against malaria and cystic fibrosis may enable the gene protein to function at lower temperatures. Therefore people who are carriers of a recessive genetic condition or even have a genetic disorder do not necessarily have more gene mutations than apparently healthy individuals.

A second example is the ambiguous concept of 'risk'. In epidemiology 'risk' is defined in relation to a population. This sort of definition is useful for public health programmes when screening is possible in the absence of cheap, risk-free diagnostic tests. 'High risk' is one that justifies the offer of a diagnostic test or management protocol which can be costly and have undesirable side-effects. In the case of antenatal screening, diagnostic tests carry an increased risk of miscarriage to the pregnancy, as well as being expensive. In the case of increased risk of breast cancer, women are offered regular mammographies and check-ups. However, the definition of what figure is 'high risk' is variable. In the absence of a national policy, it is often dependent on the financial capabilities of the local health authority. One health authority may offer people further services if their risk is between 1 in 2 and 1 in 300, whilst another may be more financially restrained and offer further services if risks are between 1 in 2 and 1 in 100.

The absolute state of risk anyone has is either 0 or 1; either the person will never have the condition or will definitely have or develop it. However, 'susceptibility' is a combination of factors associated with a disorder such that if the intensity or frequency of the factor(s) change the frequency of the disorder would also change.

For people seeking testing, their expectation often includes the existence of an accurate test that gives information that will help in making future decisions. An often confusing addition is dealing with tests whose results give risk estimates. Risk is an abstract concept for many people. Another factor to consider is that perception of risk can vary a great deal between individuals. For example, two people with a risk of 1 in 100 may view the same figure as follows:

- Very high: the person plays the lottery every week where the chance of being a winner is 1 in several millions, yet there is an expectation of being *that one*.
- Low: it is 99 to 1 that it won't happen.

Risk makes uncertainty more certain by quantifying it. A person may think they have a 'small' chance of inheriting a condition in the family, but by being given a risk, for instance of 1 in 367, that 'small' risk has been quantified. At the end of the day, screening does not give absolute answers, and cannot identify *who* out of

367 individuals will develop or inherit the disorder. This uncertainty should be balanced with the expectation of patients who come for genetic testing for an accurate prediction.

Effects and side-effects of genetic services

Before we proceed to the problem of prioritisation, one preliminary question still remains to be answered: The potential *effects* and *side-effects* of genetic counselling, testing and screening programmes. Success in these services is difficult to define and therefore to measure. In the literature several approaches have been proposed. First, is to measure *individual client outcomes*, which is not very suitable, according to Clarke, 'because they prejudge the reasons for seeking genetic counselling and how information gained in such counselling should be used'.[13] A second measure is to focus on *client satisfaction*. Two problems have been observed in this approach. First, negative information received during the counselling session may lead clients to stigmatise the service as unsatisfactory. Second, unrealistic patient expectations of diagnostic certainty may also prevent client satisfaction being used as a criterion of effectiveness. Michie *et al.* found that patients coming for genetic counselling expected information, reassurance, advice and help in making decisions.[14] When patients' expectations of reassurance and advice were met, they were less concerned and their anxiety level was lower than when these needs were not met. However, satisfying their expectations was not associated with a forecast of a better outcome.

A third approach relies on *population outcomes*. This is a highly controversial kind of measurement, especially in relation to prenatal screening programmes. This is simply because it would be unfair – and, according to Clarke, 'profoundly disrespectful to so many people with genetic conditions'[15] – to let public health policy define success in terms of primary prevention (or prevention of affected children from being born) and by how much public expenditure is reduced.

A problem of a more fundamental nature in measuring effectiveness of genetic counselling, testing and screening programmes relates to the early developmental stage of most of these programmes. That is, although we had been able to sort out the problems in the three different approaches of measuring effectiveness discussed above, it must be acknowledged that most of these test 'services' still are in the hands of researchers. Consequently, it is also too early for most of these programmes to be transformed into wider, and un-monitored, clinical practice.

The evidence for this is in several recent studies on predictive genetic testing for cancer risk. A. M. Codori, in his review article on psychological effects and side-effects in predictive genetic testing for cancer risk, writes: 'the screening and interventions that are useful in the general population remain to be shown effective in those with high genetic cancer risk'.[16]

A similar view of precaution and need for further research is expressed by Nayfield,[17] who says, 'the American Society of Human Genetics advise DNA testing for presymptomatic identification of cancer risk only in the setting of a carefully monitored research environment'.[18]

G. M. Petersen draws attention to the drawbacks of trying to assess the effect of genetic counselling and predictive testing too soon, saying that '[m]ore research is needed to optimally translate this framework into wider clinical practice'.[19] In a policy paper of the National Society of Genetic Counselors, it is stated that much uncertainty surrounds the molecular biology, appropriate medical management for gene mutation carriers and the psychological aspects of genetic testing for predisposition for late-onset disorders. According to NSGC, testing should therefore, whenever possible, be offered 'in the context of research protocols and systematic data collection, in hopes of addressing such uncertainties'.[20] Finally, in a review article on the number of people who need to be screened for a given duration to prevent one death, Rembold states that more clinical trials are needed to show the efficacy of screening strategies; this would enable the clinician to prioritise screening strategies. Today, he says, '[t]oo often politics, rather than evidence, dictates the national strategy for disease screening'.[21]

Norms of prioritisation

Norway was the first country in the world to provide a system of priorities.[22] In various forms other states and countries (Oregon, 1991; The Netherlands, 1991; Sweden, 1991–5; New Zealand, 1992; Finland, 1994 and Denmark, 1996) have followed similar models, at least in defining a core set of principles (*severity* of the disease, *effectiveness, cost-effectiveness*, and *need*) by which prioritisation decisions should be made. In the 1997 public inquiry on priority problems in Norwegian health care,[23] experiences from these alternative systems are taken into account, resulting in a somewhat less centralised system. The Norwegian system was originally based on five distinct categories of health services, which are given here:

1 *First priority* is for interventions which are necessary in the sense that failure to act will have immediate, life-threatening consequences for the patient, or groups of patients, or for society as a whole.
2 *Second priority* is for interventions which are necessary in the sense that failure will have disastrous or very grave consequences for the patient, or groups of patients, or society as a whole.
3 *Third priority* is for interventions of well-documented utility or efficacy, and where the consequences of failure are clearly undesirable but not as serious as in (1) or (2).
4 *Fourth priority* is for interventions which are in demand and are presumed to promote health and quality of life, and where the consequences of failure are clearly less serious than in (1)–(3).
5 *Fifth (or zero) priority* is for interventions which are in demand and which are neither necessary nor of well-documented utility.

In the public inquiry on prioritisation in Norway beginning on 15 May 1997, the classification of measures was based upon the same fundamental principles of *equal access*, *severity* of the disease and *effectiveness* as in the 1987 report, but also included the principle of *cost-effectiveness*. In the 1997 report it was also urged that more emphasis should be given to the principles of *effectiveness* and *cost-effectiveness* than in the 1987 guidelines.

Prioritising genetic tests and screening programmes

If we now apply these core principles to genetic testing and screening programmes, the guidelines would be as follows:

- the condition tested for is a serious one. How 'serious' is understood, and who decides, should be settled beforehand;
- the test or screening programme complies with the principles of effectiveness and cost-effectivenesss. Thus only tests with established proof of effectiveness and acceptable side-effects – economic side-effects included – ought to be offered. This seems to imply that before moving out of research laboratories and into 'the commercial laboratories' genetic tests should undergo a scientific quality control similar to that required for

drugs before marketing. For the time being no genetic test – or screening programme for that matter – seems to comply with these requirements. Otherwise spoken, existing genetic tests and screening programmes seem only to comply with the requirements of priority level 5, *i.e.* those kind of interventions which are in demand by some people and which are neither necessary nor of well documented utility;

- the genetic test or screening programme is made available to *all* who may profit medically from it.

Notes

1 Luhmann, N., *Risk: A Sociological Theory*, trans. R. Barrett, Berlin, New York: Walter de Gruyter, 1993, p. viii.
2 Ibid., p. x.
3 Clarke, A., 'Genetic counselling', *Encyclopaedia of Applied Ethics*, vol. 2, San Diego: Academic Press, 1998, pp. 391–405.
4 Wald, N. J., *The Epidemiological Approach*, 3rd edn, London: Wolfson Institute of Preventive Medicine, 1996, p. 23.
5 Weber, M., *The Protestant Ethic and the Spirit of Capitalism*, New York: Charles Scribner's Sons, 1958, p. 182.
6 National Society of Genetic Counselors, *The Code of Ethics for Genetic Counselors*, 1991.
7 Clarke, 'Genetic counselling', p. 401.
8 Ibid.
9 Ibid.
10 Ibid.
11 Ibid.
12 Bartels, D. M., Lê Roy, B. S., McCarthy, P. and Caplan, A., 'Nondirectiveness in genetic counseling: a survey of practitioners', *American Journal of Medical Genetics* 72 (1997), pp. 172–9.
13 Clarke, 'Genetic counselling', p. 399.
14 Michie, S., Bron, F., Bobrow, M. and Marteau, T., 'Nondirectiveness in genetic counselling: an empirical study', *American Journal of Human Genetics* 60 (1997), pp. 40–7.
15 Clarke, 'Genetic ccounselling', p. 399.
16 Codori, A. M., Petersen, G. M., Boyd, P. A., Brandt, J., Giardiello, F. M., 'Genetic testing for cancer in children: short-term psychological effect', *Arch Pediatr Adolesc Med* 150/11 (1996), pp. 1131–8.
17 Nayfield, S. G., 'Ethical and scientific considerations for chemoprevention research in cohorts at genetic risk for breast cancer', *J Cell Biochem Suppl* 25 (1996), pp. 123–30.
18 See Shattuck-Eidens, D., Oliphant, A., McClure, M., McBride, C., Gupte, J., Rubano, T., Pruss, D., Tavtigian, S. V., Teng, D. H., Adey, N., Staebell, M., Gumpper, K., Lundstrom, R., Hulick, M., Kelly, M., Holmen, J., Lingenfelter, B., Manley, S., Fujimura, F., Luce, M., Ward, B., Cannon-Albright, L., Steele, L., Offit, K.,

Thomas, A., *et al.*, 'BRCA1 sequence analysis in women at high risk for susceptibility mutations: risk factor analysis and implications for genetic testing', *JAMA* 278/15 (1997), pp. 1242–50.

19 Petersen, G. M., 'Genetic counseling and predictive testing for colorectal cancer risk', *Int J Cancer* 69/1 (1996), pp. 53–4. See also Giardiello, F. M., 'Genetic testing in hereditary colorectal cancer', *JAMA* 278 (1997), pp. 1278–81.

20 National Society of Genetic Counselors, 'Predisposition genetic testing for late-onset disorders in adults. *JAMA* 278/15 (1997), pp. 1217–20.

21 Rembold, C. M. 'Number needed to screen: development of a statistic for disease screening', *British Medical Journal* 317/1 (1998), pp. 307–12.

22 Norway's Public Inquiry 1987, *Guidelines for Priorities within the Norwegian Health Care System* ('Retningslinjer for prioriteringer innen norsk helsetjeneste') (NOU (Noreges offentlige utredninger); Oslo, 1987, p. 23.

23 Norway's Public Inquiry 1997, *Prioritisation revisited: a review of guidelines for prioritisations in the Norwegian Health Service* ('Prioritering på ny. Gjennomgang av retningslinjer for prioriteringer innen norsk helsetjeneste'), NOU (Noreges offentlige utredninger), Oslo, 1997, p. 18.

8

ANTENATAL SCREENING

Corinne Camilleri-Ferrante

Introduction

The issues around antenatal screening are immense, encompassing as they do questions about our attitudes to ourselves as persons, to the possibilities of a God and to the very foundations of our moral and ethical values. As antenatal care and screening have developed, people have come to expect that they will have a perfect child. But even if this were a possibility (which it is not) would it be right? It cannot be accepted that, because something is scientifically possible, it is good in itself.

All screening has the ethical basis that whatever we do we must not do harm. However, this basic ethic is immediately challenged when we are dealing with antenatal screening as a result of which parents may choose to terminate the pregnancy. It seems to me that antenatal screening that results in appropriate treatment for mother and child (e.g. Hepatitis B screening) is relatively uncontroversial, although it does raise ethical issues about the responsible use of scarce resources. Common ethical issues for screening programmes are covered in other chapters. Here, therefore, I shall concentrate on the ethical dilemmas raised by antenatal screening that may lead to termination of pregnancy.

The basis of screening is that we offer people the choice of being tested to establish whether or not they are likely to have the condition in question, which leads to diagnosis and choices of treatment. This leads to benefit for the person concerned, and sometimes for the population, in that it can reduce mortality and the burden of illness. In the case of antenatal screening, however, we are dealing not with one life but with two, mother and foetus, and what is best for one is not necessarily best for the other. We are, therefore, often faced with a dilemma, where the balance of benefit and harm have to be weighed for a number of individuals or for the population as a whole. The overriding principle that has underpinned antenatal screening is that the needs, and indeed wishes, of the mother or the parents are paramount. But is this an ethically justifiable position? This question leads to a series of ethical issues.

When is the foetus a person?

Hominization is the term used to refer to the process whereby animal consciousness changes into typical human rational self-consciousness. In evolutionary terms, it is the point at which the presence and functioning of a rational life-principle (or soul, in theological terms) occurred. How and where this happened has been the subject of heated debate for decades. However, we are faced with a similar problem for each of us as an individual. The question is 'when did "I" as "I" begin?' And does that 'personhood' confer any human rights before birth?

It must be said immediately that the answer to that question in law is 'no'. The natural meaning of the word person is restricted in law to mean a human individual who is alive after birth. This is the meaning used when defining legal rights and protection. The unborn child has no legal rights under the law. However, for the purposes of this discussion we may disregard this legal interpretation. The issue before us is when a human individual begins, not legal definitions. The fact that many governments, at various times in history, have chosen to make subsections of the population non-persons on the basis of their colour, their gender, their faith or their sexual orientation, does not change the fact that they are all human persons.

The question of 'personhood' has been a matter of debate since the earliest philosophers. Aristotle took the view that the male foetus had a sensitive soul at 40 days and the female foetus at 90 days, but that the rational soul appeared later by some mysterious divine intervention.[1] This was based upon a misunderstanding of the facts of embryology, as we know them today. There is no doubt, however, that Aristotle required some actual formation of sense organs for the presence of the life-principle.[2] These views remained unchallenged for almost two thousand years, and acquired additional weight by being substantially accepted by Thomas Aquinas, the outstanding philosopher and theologian.

Aquinas accepted most of Aristotle's thinking, although he emphasised the unity of soul and body more than Aristotle did.[3] He also differs from Aristotle in concluding that the final stage of formation is always complete by 40 days, with the creation of the intellective soul within the embryo. Ford has ably discussed all the arguments put forward by both Aristotle and Aquinas.[4] He also reviews the biblical evidence and concludes that:

> The bible does not even ask the question of the moment of the rational ensoulment or the beginning of the individual human being in the womb of the mother. An answer is not given in the Bible and should not be sought there. In other words, the Scriptures do not exempt us from our duty to continue our scientific investigations and philosophical reflections in search of a solution to the pressing question of when each one of us began to be a human individual.[5]

The teachings of the Catholic Church have, likewise, evolved. The Church has always taught the immorality of abortion at any stage after conception, but its view as to when rational ensoulment occurs has changed. Grisez suggests that the Church's view was that ensoulment occurred at 'quickening', a view lasting until 1869, when Pope Pius IX declared it incorrect.[6] However, in 1588 Pope Sixtus V had already accepted that culpability attached to abortion at any stage. Modern Catholic teaching affirms the sanctity of life from conception and was forcefully stated in the Declaration on Procured Abortion (1974), where paragraph 12 states:

> In reality respect for human life is called for from the time that the process of generation begins. From the time that the ovum is fertilised, a life is begun which is neither that of the father nor of the mother; it is rather the life of a new human being with its own growth. It would never be made human if it were not human already.[7]

Despite differences in the specifics of exactly when hominisation occurs, it is clear that those thinkers who have ascribed personhood to the foetus before birth tend to place the start of that personhood early in foetal life. Indeed, the consensus of opinion has become earlier rather than later, with debate now focusing on the need or otherwise for some functioning brain tissue. Some bioethicists feel that humanity cannot be ascribed to an organism without the potential for thought (i.e. some brain tissue) while others feel that this is immaterial since the same 'person' is demonstrably present.

There is, however, a contrary view and that is that the foetus is, at best, a potential person or, as H. Tristram Engelhardt suggests, the foetus has a certain probability of developing into a person.[8] It is clear that by this thinking, neocortical activity is necessary, but not sufficient, for the presence of a human person. For Engelhardt, personhood is dependent not only on the ability for rational thought, but also on a minimal moral sense and the ability to make choices. He says:

> Foetuses, infants, the profoundly mentally retarded, and the hopelessly comatose provide examples of human non-persons. They are members of the human species but do not in and of themselves have standing in the secular moral community.[9]

In general secular terms, then, these beings, who are of the human species and who have a great probability of developing into moral agents have a special place, but this does not, according to this school of thought, require that they be accorded the rights and standing of persons. Engelhardt goes on to suggest that:

> It is for these reasons in general secular morality that the value of zygotes, embryos, and foetuses is to be primarily understood in terms of the values they have for actual persons.[10]

The issue was debated again at length by the Warnock Committee, a committee set up by the British Government of the day to debate the ethical and moral issues around the experimentation on early human embryos and other issues arising at the very beginning of life, prior to the government enacting legislation. The Warnock Committee was largely interested in the very early, pre-implantation, embryo. The committee agreed that they could not decide when the human person began and therefore went straight to the question of how it is right to treat the human embryo.[11] It did not recognise the human embryo as a human being, but it did recommend 'That the embryo of the human species should be afforded some protection in law'.[12]

It is clear from the deliberations of the committee that they recognised the very real difficulties that would arise were the foetus to be granted full human status under the law. This would raise multiple issues about how to treat any miscarriage and whether a woman could be prosecuted for taking undue risks with her pregnancy if it subsequently miscarried. Nevertheless, the concept of providing some protection under the law, and the limits that should be placed on this, have never been fully discussed. The Warnock Committee argued that there was a balance to be struck between the rights of the foetus and those of the parents, and that the foetus should be partially protected. It is the limits of that protection that remain such a contentious issue.

One issue, which is frequently raised in this regard, is that of the potential person. Ford discusses the exact meaning of this, when he states that: 'Life itself, while being an actual characteristic, is at one and the same time itself potential, i.e. it has the inherent active potency for further life.'[13] The egg and the sperm are not 'potential persons' in the same way, since neither is an actual person and without fertilisation, neither can become a person. But '[o]nce fertilisation has taken place, a genetically human, new living individual is formed, that has the proximate potential to develop into a mature human person with the same genetic constitution.'[14] The moral significance of the embryo results from the fact that it was formed from human gametes and is naturally destined to become a human person.

However, this concentration on the personhood of the foetus has also been questioned. Both Dworkin and Kitcher have argued that centring the debate on the personhood of the foetus misses fundamental issues. Instead, it is suggested that we should recognise that differences about the legitimacy of abortion are traceable to alternative conceptions of the value of human lives.[15]

There remains, then, a difference of opinion, both about the personhood of the foetus and about the relevance of that personhood to this discussion. There are other ethical bases that are put forward as justifying antenatal screening and the consequent termination of affected pregnancies. These will now be discussed.

Screening for quality control

Evelyn Fox Keller pointed out that 'prevention means preventing the births of individuals diagnosed as genetically aberrant – in a word, it means abortion.'[16] This has frequently been justified on the grounds that many of the conditions for which we are screening allow lives of such poor quality that it is more merciful to allow no life at all. The philosopher Philip Kitcher suggests that: 'Utopian eugenics treats abortion as one among many medical techniques for reducing human suffering.'[17]

The problem arises in deciding which parameters should be used to judge quality of life. Our ideas have changed radically through the centuries. Thus Aristotle believed that life should be judged by our ability to develop our natural talents. The Church Fathers believed that lives should be judged by their spiritual development and closeness to God. During the Enlightenment, intellect was all, while the Romantics rebelled against that and were fulfilled by deep emotions. Some, or all, of these things influence our thinking today. Philip Kitcher has recently suggested that quality of life should be judged in three dimensions:

> The first focuses on whether the person has developed any sense of what is significant and how the conception of what matters was formed. The second assesses the extent to which those desires that are central to the person's life plan are satisfied: Did the person achieve those things that mattered most? Finally, the third is concerned with the character of the person's experience, the balance of pleasure and pain.[18]

In propounding his first dimension, Kitcher proposes that the inability for any self-development is incompatible with a life of any value and thus that such an affected foetus may justifiably be aborted. He gives the example of Tay-Sachs Disease and says:

> Doctors, parents, even many religious leaders agree on the permissibility of terminating pregnancies when the foetus is diagnosed as positive for Tay-Sachs, not because the baby will suffer pain – that can relatively easily be avoided – but because neurodegeneration will start before the distinctive life of an individual person can begin.[19]

Most contemporary bioethicists would agree with Kitcher's view that, faced with a foetus with a known (severe) defect, termination is morally justifiable. Some have gone further, and called it morally obligatory. Margery Shaw has suggested that parents who knowingly give birth to a seriously impaired child are guilty of negligent child abuse.[20]

The opposing view is put by Brock L. Eide, who points out that these quality of life criteria could equally well be used to justify the killing of severely handicapped infants and mentally impaired children and adults, or even to justify abortion for sex selection in countries where females have a clearly lower quality of life. He continues: 'Indeed, such subjective third party assessments of quality of life are unavoidably elastic, capable of being stretched to accommodate whatever concerns or biases the assessor might have.'[21]

Perhaps this view was even more simply put by Leon Kass, when he stated that, 'the principle "defectives should not be born" is a principle without limits.'[22] Brock quotes the religious ethicist Allen Verhey who has said:

> There are, I think, genetic conditions like Tay-Sachs which consign a child not only to an abbreviated life, but to a life subjectively indistinguishable from torture; and there are conditions like trisomy 18 which are inconsistent not only with life but with the minimal conditions for human communication. Prenatal diagnosis and abortion, I think, can be used responsibly.[23]

Brock goes on to point out that this argument must entail either an acceptance of other life-taking practices, such as infanticide or euthanasia, or the devaluation of prenatal human life.

There is an additional question, which is rarely addressed in this context, and that is, how severe does the abnormality have to be? We have seen that there are some conditions, such as Tay-Sachs, where the majority opinion is in favour of termination. Even if one accepts this, however, does the same hold true for Down's Syndrome or cystic fibrosis? The former condition is associated with mental retardation, of varying severity, and with other congenital defects. However, people with Down's Syndrome can, and do, give and receive a lot of love, and live lives which appear to be fulfilled within their own limitations. This is even more true for cystic fibrosis sufferers, whose life expectancy at birth is now of the order of 40 years, and who live essentially normal lives, yet who are faced with the knowledge that they are likely to die young and they require considerable medical intervention throughout their lives. Is this sufficient reason to deprive them of that life, or should the purpose of quality control be not to attain some perfect 'normal' standard, but the best quality of life which can be achieved for that particular person?

Whose benefit?

As we have seen, the 'benefit' to the foetus is, at best, debatable, depending as it does on the subjective, third-party, decision that that particular life would not be worth living. There are, however, benefits to be gained by the family and society at large; they might be termed the 'population perspective'.

The argument for family benefit is that the birth of a severely handicapped child places enormous strains on the other family members, thus reducing the quality of their life. This is essentially a balancing of one life against another and an accepting that the foetal life is of less intrinsic value than the lives of those it will affect. Kitcher makes the point:

> Liberals about abortion take the value of human lives to arise as the result of human investment in those lives. In consequence, they view the continuation of some pregnancies as greatly diminishing the value of lives – the lives of parents, children already born, others who are affected – in which there has already been substantial human investment, and see this diminution of value as a far greater loss than the cessation of a human life that has not yet begun in earnest.[24]

Eide takes a different view, arguing that many families who have experience of a handicapped child have found it deeply enriching and that it is impossible to know what would be truly best for each individual family.[25] Despite this, I believe it is unarguable that few, if any, families would choose to have a handicapped child and it would be pointless to suggest that, despite the great rewards that can be reaped, there is not also considerable suffering. I believe that the issue here is one of the balance between benefit and harm. The question to be debated should be, 'Does the benefit of not having a handicapped child in the family outweigh the harm of terminating a pregnancy?' And the answer to that question depends upon the value that is placed on individual human lives at any stage of development.

A similar argument is put forward about the benefit to society, although this is a more openly utilitarian one. The argument is that the disabled consume a greater share of society's resources and that they yield little or no benefit to the rest of society. All these arguments, although often repeated, have little solid evidence.

It is extremely difficult to include all the costs on each side of the equation, particularly when one includes the costs incurred by a 'normal' child, who often 'replaces' the 'defective' one.[26]

There is also a potential problem in that terminating affected pregnancies might actually increase the frequency of disease alleles. Marc Lappe, quoted by Eide, has written that:

> the process of aborting a foetus with a deleterious recessive disease and then compensating for the loss of the expected child by trying to have more children ultimately results in a subtle increase in frequency of the recessive gene over many generations. This is true because with reproductive compensation, two-thirds of all of the live children will be carriers of the recessive gene at issue, instead of the one half normally expected without prenatal diagnosis.[27]

Whose choice?

It has often been stated that screening is ethically justifiable because it gives information and allows informed choice. There can be no argument against this when it leads to an improvement in the care of the mother and her baby, as in the case of Hepatitis B screening or screening for HIV. However, ignoring for one moment the issue of what choice there is (i.e., can it ever be theoretically justifiable to produce information for a choice that is itself ethically dubious?), once again, the issue of benefit against harm is still present.

Screening tests do not produce a final diagnosis; they identify a high-risk group who must then undergo a diagnostic test. This is well illustrated by Down's Syndrome screening. The initial test identifies those pregnancies at higher risk (an arbitrary cut-off point of 1 : 250 or 300) of having Down's Syndrome. Those women are then offered amniocentesis. The majority of these pregnancies will, in fact, turn out not to have trisomy 21. Unfortunately, amniocentesis carries with it a miscarriage rate of 1–2 per cent. Therefore, for each baby identified with Down's Syndrome another, normal, baby is lost through miscarriage.[28] The debate which society needs to have is whether or not it is ethical to submit pregnancies to this kind of risk, in order to allow 'informed choice'.

This raises the next question: 'whose informed choice?' There is more than one life here: there is the mother, and usually the father and possibly other family members, but there is also the foetus. And she cannot give 'informed consent'.

Our current ethical thought seems to be predicated on the owner-ship of the foetus by her mother or parents. Engelhardt has written that:

> one also owns what one produces . . . The fact that young children will become persons, limits the extent to which parents have ownership rights over their young children. However, these limits will be very weak . . . with regard to ownership rights in human zygotes, embryos and foetuses that will not be allowed to develop into persons . . . At the point that an entity becomes self-conscious, the morality of permission or mutual respect would alienate the property rights of the parents over their children.[29]

This, of course, is not a new idea, being embedded in Roman law, but more recently it has been questioned. The philosopher John Locke argued that such views are fundamentally flawed[30] and his view was very influential in western thought. Indeed, the concept that he raises of parental duty, rather than right, is one that under-pins the current Children Act.[31] However, this view is not one that prevails in regard to the foetus, where the concept of parental ownership and rights seems, once again, to be prevalent.

Engelhardt suggests that

> If a human foetus has more than the moral status of an animal with a similar level of development, in general secular terms it will be because of the significance of that life for the woman who has conceived it, for others around her who may be interested in it, and for the future person it may become. As incongruous as this comparison of animals and human foetuses will appropriately appear to those who with religious faith understand the evil of abortion, it is a comparison affirmed in secular criminal codes that allow women to abort their foetuses, but not torture their pets.[32]

Implied in this view is the idea that the zygote or foetus is the un-disputed property of the parents, particularly the mother. It is essen-tially private property, with the mother having the right to do with it what she will within the limits of the law. This also, however, makes it improper to use force – whether mental, physical or psychological – to determine the abortion choices of a woman.[33]

For there are also other players in this situation – the medical profession. The concept that doctors have any right to interfere in a mother's choice is one that I believe most people would find morally unacceptable. Yet the truth of the situation is that they do heavily influence parental choice, both in the way in which choices are presented to the parents and in what exactly parents are told. Thus, doctors take an arbitrary cut-off for what constitutes a high risk pregnancy for Down's Syndrome, and present the mother who has a risk of 1 in 250 with the opinion that she ought to have an amniocentesis but the mother with a risk of 1 in 275 with the information that her test did not show her to be at high risk. Many women have reported being presented with a test result that required them to make a 'choice' about amniocentesis, and possibly termination, when they had not understood the purpose of the first screening test, nor fully appreciated the risks associated with amniocentesis.[34] Despite the anecdotal nature of many of these reports, they present a concern about how and when women are asked to make difficult choices. There is also evidence from a survey carried out by the National Childbirth Trust, and from anecdotal evidence, that many women found to be at 'high risk' are then pressurised into having the amniocentesis and even into taking the decision to abort. It has even been suggested that women ought to be made to decide that they will have a termination prior to the amniocentesis. This calls into question the entire possibility of an ethical argument based on choice. Surely, the carers of a pregnant woman cannot be perceived as having the ethical right to force her into any choice.

In conclusion

Ultimately, ethics is not an absolute science, but a debate about which society must reach some consensus. The debate over whether or not there is such a thing as natural law has recently been reopened by the work of Finnis and Grisez.[35] They have re-examined the work of Aquinas and are strongly suggesting that he has been ill served by his followers and that the natural law does exist. The subject is far too large for this chapter, but may throw more light on this issue as the debate continues.

Calabresi and Bobbitt stated: 'a moral society must depend on moral conflict as the basis for determining morality.'[36] And therein lies the danger, for societies can, and do, get things terribly wrong. Our century has produced adequate proof of that. In this chapter I have attempted to put forward the differing views, all so passionately held, which are expressed on this subject. Finally, however, the whole argument seems to me to hinge on the value that we are prepared to place on the life of an unborn child and on the balance between benefit and harm, and to whom. Society needs to debate these issues openly, but honestly, since the benefits and harm of antenatal screening remain open to question and debate. Finally, I return once again to Engelhardt: 'No matter how truly one knows the evils of abortion and infanticide, this cannot be established in general secular moral terms.'[37]

Notes

1 The works of Aristotle translated in English, vol. IV, *The History of Animals*, eds J. A. Smith and W. D. Ross, trans. by D. W. Thompson, Oxford: Oxford University Press, 1967, p. 583.
2 Aristotle, *On The Soul* (De anima), tr. W. S. Hett, London and Cambridge, Mass.: Heinemann, 1957, p. 142.
3 Aquinas, *Summa Theologiae*, vol. II, ed. and tr. T. Suttor, 1a, 76, 4 ad 1. London: Blackfriars/Eyre & Spottiswoode.
4 N.M. Ford, *When Did I Begin?*, Cambridge: Cambridge University Press, 1988.
5 Ibid., p. 57.
6 G. Grisez, *Abortion: The Myths, the Realities and the Arguments*, New York: Corpus Book, World Publishing Company, 1972, p. 177.
7 *Declaration on Procured Abortion*, Vatican, 1974.
8 H. Tristram Engelhardt Jr., *The Foundations of Bioethics*, 2nd edn, Oxford: Oxford University Press, 1996, p. 142.
9 Ibid., p. 139.
10 Ibid., p. 143.
11 *Report of the Committee of Inquiry into Human Fertilisation and Embryology*, Chairman, Dame Mary Warnock, Dept. Health and Social Security, London: HMSO, 1984, p. 60, 11–15.
12 Ibid., p. 63, 11–17.
13 N. M. Ford, *When Did I Begin?*, Cambridge: Cambridge University Press, 1988, p. 96.
14 Ibid., p. 97.
15 Philip Kitcher, *The Lives to Come*, New York: Simon and Schuster, 1996, p. 229.
16 Evelyn Fox Keller, 'Nature, nurture and the human Genome project', in *The Code of Codes*, eds Daniel J. Kelves and Leroy Hood, Cambridge, Mass.: Harvard University Press, 1992, p. 296.
17 Kitcher, *The Lives to Come*, p. 224.
18 Ibid., p. 289.
19 Ibid., p. 288.

20 Margery W. Shaw, 'The potential plaintiff: preconception and prenatal torts, in *Genetics and the Law II*, eds Aubrey Milinsky and George J. Annas, New York: Plenum, 1980, pp. 225–32.
21 Brock L. Eide, 'The least a parent can do: prenatal genetic testing and the welcome of our children', *Ethics and Medicine* 13:3 (1997), pp. 59–66.
22 Leon R. Kass, *Toward a More Natural Science: Biology and Human Affairs*, New York: Free Press, 1985, p. 89.
23 Allen Verhey, transcript of a talk given at the Christian Stake in Genetics Conference, July 1996, quoted in Eide, 'The least a parent can do'.
24 Kitcher, *The Lives to Come* p. 229.
25 Eide, 'The least a parent can do'.
26 Kass, *Toward a More Natural Science*, p. 92.
27 Eide, 'The least a parent can do'.
28 N. J. Wald, Anne Kennard, A. Hackshaw, Ali McGuire. 'Antenatal screening for Down's Syndrome', *Journal of Medical Screening* 4 (1997), pp. 181–246.
29 Engelhardt, *Foundations of Bioethics*, p. 156.
30 John Locke, *An Essay Concerning the True Original Extent and End of Civil Government*, Chicago: Encyclopaedia Britannica, p. 36.
31 The Children Act 1989 as amended.
32 Engelhardt, *Foundations of Bioethics*, p. 255.
33 Ibid., p. 256.
34 Josephine Treloar, 'The cradle of the womb', *FAITH Magazine*, Jan.–Feb. 1998.
35 John Finnis, *Natural Law and Natural Rights*, Clarendon Law Series, Oxford: Clarendon Press, 1980. G. Grisez and J. Finnis, 'The basic principles of natural law: a reply to Ralph McInerny', *American Journal of Jurisprudence* 26 (1981), pp. 21–31.
36 G. Calabresi and P. Bobbitt, *Tragic Choices*, New York: Norton, 1978, p. 198.
37 Engelhardt, *Foundations of Bioethics*, p. 257.

9

CHILDHOOD SCREENING

Sarah Stewart-Brown

Introduction

This chapter examines the ethical base of current childhood screening programmes, which are amongst the oldest of the screening programmes currently provided by the UK National Health Service. Some of the problems raised are similar to those of neonatal and adult screening programmes, others are unique. The most important ethical problem with these programmes is that the process of identifying the benefits and harms is complicated and incomplete, but this information is not communicated to parents. Parents may therefore make the decision to bring their children for screening on the basis of false assumptions. Some of the reasons why the value of these programmes has not been challenged until the late 1980s are explored together with some potential solutions to improving the ethical base of future programmes.

The origins of childhood screening

Childhood screening programmes have a long history, longer than that of most other screening programmes and the aims of these programmes have changed over time. This is important in the context of a discussion about the ethics of screening because the ethical basis of an intervention must depend in part on what those who are offering the intervention aim to achieve and on the extent to which their aim is achieved in practice. These programmes have their origins in the school medical service, set up in the early part of the twentieth century in the aftermath of the Boer War. The level of physical fitness amongst potential recruits to the armed forces in this war was sufficiently low to be a cause of national concern (see Report of the Interdepartmental Committee on Physical Deterioration,

1904). The Education Act of 1907 required local authorities to carry out medical inspections on all children in school so that in future the level and cause of disease and disability in the population could be determined, and population health monitored. Routine medical examination or 'surveillance' of babies and pre-school children developed in the latter half of the century with a different goal.[1] This service aimed to identify children with special educational needs so that the education service could be notified in advance and children could receive early educational interventions if appropriate. In both programmes the aim of identifying children who might benefit from health services interventions to reduce disability, evolved over time.

Differences between childhood and adult screening programmes

Childhood screening programmes present a contrast with later screening programmes in a number of other ways. First, as they grew out of general medical inspections in which children were examined 'to see if there was anything wrong with them' these programmes differ from programmes established to reduce morbidity or mortality from specific diseases. Childhood pre-school and school medical examinations still aim to detect a range of problems.

Second, the goal of these programmes is usually to detect diseases causing disability rather than life-threatening conditions. The health impact of conditions which cause disability is intrinsically more difficult to establish than that of fatal conditions, making the measurement of health gain from screening more of a challenge. Third, whereas the therapeutic goal of most later programmes is to reverse the disease process and restore health (secondary prevention), the goal of many childhood screening programmes is to ameliorate disability or handicap rather than to prevent it (tertiary prevention). Finally the responsibility for children's health care rests with parents and in the evaluation of childhood screening programmes it is often the parents who are required to judge the benefit and harms rather than the children themselves. It is parents who need to make the time to enable their children to attend screening and it is parents who suffer the anxiety that follows a positive screening result. So some of the harms which are attributable to screening primarily affect parents rather than children.

The ethical issues in childhood screening programmes arise both from the way in which these programmes differ from other programmes and from the things they have in common. The first and most important of the latter is that screening programmes should do more good than harm. Screening programmes which do not fulfil this criterion fail to stand up to critical scrutiny in all ethical frameworks. Defining and measuring 'good' and 'harm' can however be surprisingly complex.

The primary good that screening programmes do is attributable to reduction in distress from disease, disability, handicap or premature death. This reduction may secondarily increase the ability of the disabled or diseased child to contribute to society, or reduce the need for care from society. The first step in considering the ethics of childhood screening programmes is therefore to establish the extent and nature of distress attributable to the conditions that can be identified and the benefits attributable to treatment. The second step, establishing the harm that these programmes can do is also complex, because the harm may be attributable to several factors: those intrinsic to all screening programmes, which arise as a result of false positive and false negative cases; those arising through organisational problems with the programmes, like long waiting times for diagnosis; and those related to the potential side-effects of treatment, which are condition specific. The latter are relevant to an assessment of screening programmes because the aim of screening is to identify and treat children who would not otherwise have been treated and exposed to these side-effects.

Identifing and quantifying health gain

Vision screening

The example of vision screening illustrates a number of the difficulties which can be faced in trying to estimate the health gain from childhood screening programmes.[2] The primary aim of childhood vision screening programmes is to detect amblyopia, a condition in which an anatomically normal eye loses the ability to see. Amblyopia nearly always affects only one eye and therefore does not prevent children or adults from seeing. It may be present at varying levels of severity. It may have an effect on two-dimensional perception or stereopsis. If severe, it may cause a restriction in the field of vision. It also causes problems if the other eye becomes diseased or injured. There is a strong professional belief that unioccular vision must be less good than binocular vision and that amblyopia must cause children problems. However this apparently straightforward belief does not seem to be supported by patient experience or by research evidence. One small qualitative study undertaken with adults and children who suffer from amblyopia documented the fact that some people with amblyopia are not able to identify the way in which their amblyopia has affected them.[3] This may be because uniocular vision is not disabling or because it is difficult to perceive a lack of something one has never had. Although there are doubtless some individuals who are disabled by amblyopia, identifying the benefit that might accrue from the identification and treatment of all amblyopes requires a series of research studies which have never been done.

There is a standard intervention for amblyopia which as been developed largely on the basis of studies in animals. The intervention involves correction of any refractive error and patching of the good eye to stimulate the sight in the poor eye. For over a century ophthalmologists and orthoptists have been applying this treatment, observing that the vision in the poor eye usually improves during treatment. There are however studies suggesting that at least minor degrees of amblyopia may improve spontaneously and reports of vision improving in amblyopic eyes when vision in the good eye is lost in later life. There is no population-based information about what usually happens to amblyopia in the absence of treatment (its natural history). There are also no randomised controlled trials of treatment, so it is impossible to be sure that the improvement ophthalmologists observe would not have occurred in the absence of intervention.[4]

So there is little information on the extent of disability attributable to amblyopia and the evidence base for the impact of treatment is poor. Thus it would seem that parents are invited to bring their children for vision screening on the basis of professional beliefs that this is going to benefit them. Parents and children have not been invited to contribute to the debate about whether there is any overall benefit, although they are in a better position than professionals to judge both the gain and the harm. If parents are participating in these programmes uncritically in the belief that the professionals know best what is good for children, they might be distressed if they knew the insubstantial basis of the evidence. The ethical issue here is whether it is acceptable for professionals to offer a programme which might not be acceptable to parents if they knew the truth. Suppose a parent brings a child for vision screening believing that in doing so something might be found which would if left untreated damage her child's sight; say that the orthoptist finds the child to be amblyopic and prescribes patching; say the parent finds it difficult to maintain the patching regime, but continues to patch because she believes that the child's sight will be damaged if she doesn't. In this scenario the parent might quite rightly be angry if she discovered the slender evidence relating to amblyopia and disability and the even slenderer nature of the evidence relating to the effectiveness of patching. She might feel that she had been encouraged to participate under false pretences, and that she had therefore been unable to give informed consent.

Neurodevelopmental delay

Childhood screening programmes which aim to detect untreatable neurodevelopmental delay, which may be attributable to a range of conditions, are often justified on the basis that parents welcome early diagnosis.[5] Parents usually suspect abnormalities in their child before they are recognised by professionals[6] and the recognition brings relief from nagging doubts. It may be accompanied by the provision of supportive services or more simply by an empathetic response. The benefits may be quite subtle, but potentially important for the health of family members. It may be a mother who feels less guilty about giving birth to a handicapped child, or a father who feels less ashamed. It may be a family in which normal siblings do not resent the extra attention given to the disabled child, a family that can accept the death of a disabled child without guilt, or one in which family breakdown is avoided. All these potential gains would depend on the interpersonal and communication skills of the professionals running the support services. The same screening programme could be beneficial in a part of the country where the community paediatricians work in a way which is supportive and empathetic and detrimental in a part of the country where they are dismissive of parental anxieties and concerns. These factors are rarely documented or measured in trials of treatment or local service audits, so the only way of finding out whether the service is helpful would be to consult parents. This is another situation in which it might be more ethical for parents to be allowed to make a choice. If they have a realistic knowledge of what a screening programme aims to offer, they should be better placed than health professionals to decide whether it would be helpful for them.

General benefits

Childhood screening programmes are sometimes justified as a way of reaching parents or, in the school health service, teenagers. Health professionals will argue that although a screening programme may not be justifiable in its own right, it brings parents and teenagers into contact with health professionals who can then check that the child is thriving and offer useful health information. They may say that such added value could make an important difference to the health gain from programmes of marginal benefit. This argument, however, does not stand up to critical ethical scrutiny. It is essentially manipulative. If parents or children find such a contact with health professionals supportive and the information useful, they will come regardless of the offer of screening. If they would not otherwise come, they are being recruited under false pretences.

There are other marginal benefits that possibly should be added to the cost and benefit equation. Pre-school vision screening programmes occasionally identify a child with a rare treatable condition such as retinoblastoma. Such tumours are too rare to justify screening but if the programme is justified on other grounds then the finding of such tumours represents added value.

Conclusions

Quantifying the potential gain attributable to childhood screening programmes can be complex. The gain is determined not just by the extent of handicap which the condition causes, but also by the effectiveness of the interventions that can be offered. These programmes have the potential to identify several different conditions with varying degrees of efficiency and the effectiveness of interventions for the different conditions may vary. If there is no intervention, or the interventions are only partially effective in the pre-symptomatic phase, the benefits and therefore the ethics of screening must be questionable. Quantifying the potential gain is however only the starting point for establishing whether programmes do more harm than good. The gain needs to be set against the potential harm and this may be even more difficult to quantify. Failure to fully appreciate the potential harms experienced by parents and children from screening has in the past weighted the professional view firmly in favour of screening.

Identifying and quantifying harm attributable to screening

In contrast to the health gain from screening, which is usually programme specific, many of the potential harms attributable to screening are generic to all programmes. Those that are programme specific arise from the need for further diagnostic investigation and from side-effects of treatment for the disease. These side-effects may be subtle and difficult to quantify. There is no doubt that some children find treatment for amblyopia (patching) very distressing and 'compliance' with treatment is a problem.[7] The extent of this distress has never been clearly documented and its implications for considering the pros and cons of the treatment, let alone screening, are not routinely taken into account.

The 'generic harms' from childhood screening programmes arise from the fact that no screening test is perfect and all programmes generate false positive and false negative results. Identification of a child as 'screen positive' engenders anxiety and concern in parents regardless of whether the child actually has the problem. If subsequent examination or testing shows the child to be normal – in a false positive case – the anxiety does not necessarily resolve straight away.[8] Parents may wonder if it was the second investigation that was 'wrong' rather than the screening test. For these parents the screening programme has created problems and offered no benefit. Parents whose children are identified by the screening test as being normal who actually have the problem (false negative cases) may have sufficient confidence in the test to dismiss their own observations and concerns about their child. In this situation the screening process may prevent parents from doing what they would otherwise have done and as a consequence the test result may delay the start of an effective intervention. This is a problem which has been discussed most in the context of the 7–9 month hearing screening test, the infant distraction test,[9] but the extent of the problem in this and other programmes is not well researched.

School entry hearing screening

Childhood hearing screening programmes offered at school entry present examples of both generic and programme specific harms. At this age it is possible to identify a very small number of children with mild or unilateral sensineural loss, and a very large number of children who happen to be suffering at that particular moment from glue ear. Glue ear is a condition which affects two-thirds of children at some stage in their lives. During the pre-school period, one in five children are likely to have the problem at any one time. It may cause mild to moderate hearing loss, but does not do so always. As a result of intermittent episodes of mild deafness such children may suffer from being labelled as stupid. Except in a small percentage of cases the condition resolves spontaneously, but for that small percentage intervention may be very helpful.[10] The gain from this screening programme is the identification of two small groups of children whose hearing may be improved by intervention. The main harm is suffered by the large number of children with spontaneously resolving or intermittent glue ear who are required to undergo further investigation and sometimes a minor operation unnecessarily. The parents of these children suffer considerable anxiety whilst waiting for the problem to be clarified and solved. In many parts of the country this anxiety has been exacerbated by very long waiting times for investigation at Hearing and Speech Centres. These were the inevitable consequence of the high false positive rate in the screening programme. The opportunity cost of devoting professional energy to the school entry hearing screening programme may prevent the search for alternative and better solutions. For example the problems of children with glue ear might be more effectively solved by sensitising teachers and parents to the difficulties they experience, so that the latter can relate to these children in a supportive rather than critical way.

Psychological versus physical benefits and harms

One problem with balancing the benefits and harm attributable to screening programmes is the fact that the benefits can usually be measured in terms of physical health, whereas the harms are often psychological. Methods of measuring the latter are less well developed than those for measuring physical health, and physical health gain may be regarded as more important than emotional or psychological distress. Whatever their relative importance, it is widely recognised that psychological side-effects are a problem. It is for these reasons that the screening programmes that have been introduced more recently are carefully monitored, so that the level of false positive cases and the programme yield are known. Monitoring the level of false negative cases is more difficult, but an estimate can be made by comparing actual and expected programme yield. Childhood screening programmes are notable for the absence of monitoring. Some community paediatricians have recently managed to set up systems in which the results of further investigations are fed back to the child health services, but this is relatively rare. For many of these programmes the extent of the potential problems attributable to false positive and negative cases is not known.

General harmful effects

Other more subtle outcomes of the process of screening have been proposed. The need for a medical examination or screening test to detect abnormality is only necessary if professionals have observational skills or access to technological equipment which the parents lack. The availability of screening programmes therefore sends a message to parents about their own competence with regard to meeting their children's needs, relative to that of health professionals. This process therefore has the potential to disempower parents and may encourage the belief that they need to ask a professional if their child is well rather than relying on their own judgement. Disempowerment is potentially damaging to health in its own right.[11] In the above context it would also raise consultation rates and incur opportunity costs on the health service. These potential side-effects of screening programmes are plausible and potentially important. All have been documented but the extent of the problems created has not yet been seriously researched.

Conclusions

Identifying and measuring the potential harms from childhood screening programmes is therefore a complex process and one that is seriously incomplete. Attempting to balance these harms against the potential benefits, when neither have been adequately measured, is even more complex. There are concerns about the balance of benefit and harm for almost all the child health screening programmes and during the 1990s some of these programmes have been discontinued.[12] The question arises as to why it took so long for these programmes to come under serious scrutiny. Because the benefits and harms of screening depend on the severity and prevalence of the disease, and on the effectiveness of treatment, and because many of the diseases in question have changed in prevalence and severity over the course of the century and treatment has improved, it seems self-evident that the success of such programmes should be regularly appraised. It is therefore reasonable to ask, What has gone wrong?

Possible reasons for the insecure ethical basis of childhood screening programmes

Failure seriously to address health gain from childhood screening might be attributable in part to the origins of the programme. The statutory requirement for school medical inspections to be undertaken may have absolved both clinicians and public health doctors from the responsibility of thinking about whether children derived any benefit from identification of their conditions or abnormalities. Equally, the divided responsibility between public health doctors and clinicians may also have played a part. Both school and pre-school programmes were set up with the aim of monitoring population health and notifying cases. They therefore had a public health function independent of their value to individual children. While the latter function has evolved over time the public health function has now disappeared. Nevertheless, many clinicians still believe that these programmes are justified on public health grounds and that their clinical role is limited to doing their best to help children who are identified as abnormal. At the same time, public health doctors, who know that the programmes are no longer appropriate for monitoring public health, believe the interventions which follow identification are sufficiently evidence-based to justify screening. To make the allocation of responsibility more complicated still, many of the interventions which follow screening are delivered by a separate group of professionals (special needs teachers, ophthalmologists, ENT surgeons). This may also have acted as a disincentive to the framing of challenging questions about effectiveness. When responsibility for finding children is separated organisationally from the responsibility for treatment, the responsibility for considering whether the process of finding is worthwhile is easily lost.

These programmes may also have escaped scrutiny because discontinuing programmes without very strong evidence that they are ineffective or damaging is difficult. Although lack of evidence of effectiveness is a stronger argument for discontinuing screening services than it is for discontinuing clinical services (see previous chapter) the health professionals involved may still find it difficult to accept. Such professionals have usually been trained in the current paradigm and are delivering programmes in good faith. They are likely to have been encouraging parents to attend on the basis of their belief that what they have to offer is worthwhile. Parents may also find it difficult to accept that the professionals might have got it wrong. In the context of the current NHS, proposals to discontinue services are almost always interpreted as an attempt to save money. Discontinuing programmes carries implications for the employment prospects of the professionals working in the service. Where critical appraisal of the screening programme has raised doubts about treatment efficacy, as in the case of vision screening[13] these problems are exacerbated. The ethics of making redundant people who have been recruited and trained by the NHS to do a job they are currently doing well, also needs consideration. In the commercial world there would be no dilemma but the caring professions have in the past operated under a different code of practice.

Improving the ethical base

Screening programmes that are offered to parents on the implicit assumption that they will benefit their child are likely to be unethical if there are serious doubts about the balance of benefit and harm. The people running these programmes are, however, likely to be acting in good faith even though they may be misguided. Suggesting that a programme is unethical because of the inadequate evidence base may create such a furore that it becomes more, rather than less likely that the programme is discontinued. However it is still important that a way is found of moving the debate forward. One important step forward would be the commissioning of research which aims to define and quantify the benefits and harms, but this alone is unlikely to be sufficient.

In the meanwhile it is important also to consider how much it matters if parents bring their children for a screening test believing that it can offer something that it cannot. To what extent is it the professionals' responsibility to ensure that parents are making decisions on the best available evidence? The media have an important influence on what the public believe, and what they say cannot be controlled by professionals. The public's health beliefs are based on historical and lay information which is not directly the responsibility of health professionals. The question partly hinges on whether parents would make a different decision if they had the best available evidence. If this is a possibility then it must be the responsibility of the health professionals offering screening and treatment to ensure that parents know the limitations of the process and are free to make up their own minds.

To achieve this several things would have to change. Parents would need to be informed about what screening programmes had to offer and have time to consider and discuss the pros and cons without any pressure. This might not be easy; the information would certainly need to be available in several different media. Proposals are being made that the child health service move to a more health-promoting base,[14] in which education and support for parents rather than screening and the identification of abnormality are the primary goal. Because the psychological and emotional consequences of screening and treatment and the impact of potential disability are more obvious to parents than they are to health professionals, they would be better placed to make a value judgement on whether participation was worthwhile for them. Professionals would need to respect parents' decisions and not put pressure on them to attend. At present some parents take their child for screening on the basis of the belief that if they do not the professionals might regard them as uncaring parents. Such feelings may or may not be engendered by the health professionals themselves. Pressure to participate cannot be justified ethically in the face of an uncertain evidence base and is likely to distort the decisions parents make even when offered the relevant evidence.

The proposal that parents should be encouraged to choose whether to attend screening would mean that that those with limited time, energy and resources might not bring their children for screening. Although a screening programme might be able to reduce handicap it might also exacerbate other family problems, like lack of time, resources or social support. The savings made from discontinuing marginally helpful screening programmes might be used to provide social or educational programme which offer parents in such circumstances what they perceive they need.

Notes

1 Hall, D. M. B. (ed.) (1989) *Health for All Children: A Programme for Child Health Surveillance*, Oxford: Oxford University Press, p. 12.
2 Snowdon, S. K. and Stewart-Brown, S. L. (1997a) 'Pre-school vision screening'. *Health Technology Assessment Review* 1, 8.
3 Snowdon, S. K. and Stewart-Brown, S. L. (1997b) *Amblyopia and Disability: A Qualitative Study*, Oxford: Health Services Research Unit, University of Oxford.
4 Snowdon and Stewart-Brown (1997a).
5 Hall (1989).
6 Glascoe F. P. (1997) 'Parents' concerns about children's development: prescreening technique or screening test?, *Pediatrics* 99, pp. 522–8.

7 Snowden and Stewart Brown (1997b).
8 Marteau,T. M., Kidd, J., Cook, R., Johnston, M., Michie, S., Shaw, R. W. and Slack, J. (1988) 'Screening for Down's Syndrome', *British Medical Journal* 297, p. 1469; Tymstra, T. (1986) 'False positive results in screening tests: experiences of parents of children screened for congenital hypothyroidism', *Family Practice* 3, pp. 92–6.
9 Hall (1989).
10 NHS Centre for Reviews and Dissemination (1993) 'The treatment of persistent glue ear in children', *Effective Health Care Bulletin* 1, 5.
11 Wallerstein, N. (1992) 'Powerlessness, empowerment and health: implications for health promotion programmes', *American Journal of Health Promotion* 6, pp. 197–205.
12 Hall (1989); Hall, D. M. B. (ed.) (1996) *Health for All Children*, 3rd edn, Oxford: Oxford University Press.
13 Stewart-Brown, S. L. and Snowdon, S. K. (1997) 'Evidence based dilemmas in pre-school vision screening', *Archives of Disease in Childhood*, 78, pp. 406–407.
14 Hall (1996).

Part III

HEALTH PROMOTION, RESEARCH AND PUBLIC PARTICIPATION IN HEALTH CARE

In this section the issues of health promotion, research and public participation in health care decision-making are discussed. This section considers how individual interests can be balanced against potential health gain for the population.

The chapter by Burls and Cabello-López considers the particular problems for public health research and considers how ethical reflection can promote worthwhile research, whilst minimising harm to individuals. In the following chapter, by Burls, some of the issues of involving the public in decision-making and the problems in reconciling disagreements between professionals and the public are discussed. Communication to and participation by the public in health policy decision-making is seen as making an essential contribution to meaningful decisions.

The next two chapters argue the importance of the professional perspective in resolving health policy dilemmas. In the chapter by Holt, Beal and Breach the issue of compulsory fluoridation of water supplies is considered. They consider the ethical principles of beneficence, non-maleficence, autonomy and justice and argue that the measure is effective and fair, even though a minority may lose their right to choose. Monaghan considers the legal and ethical aspects of community dental screening. He concludes that dental screening is sometimes justified without positive parental consent, in order to promote the health of individual children and the population (especially in the context of health inequalities). He argues that the possiblity of parental rights being infringed is over-ridden by the potential benefit of screening to the child. In the chapter preceding his, by Bradley, asking whether childhood vaccination should be compulsory, the opposite conclusion is reached. Bradley considers rights theory and the risks and benefits of vaccination and concludes that a compulsory vaccination policy cannot be justified, since parents' views on vaccination must also carry importance.

In conclusion, there are tensions between professionals and individuals in establishing 'fair' or ethical health policy. These chapters illustrate a range of views from the more traditional professional attitudes of 'knowing best', to a more open consideration of how decision-making could be shared with the public.

10

RESEARCH METHODS IN PUBLIC HEALTH

Amanda Burls and Juan Cabello-López

Introduction

This chapter looks at the relationship between research methods in public health and bioethical principles. This subject can be viewed from two perspectives: how do bioethical principles influence the choice of research design in public health? And how can the values people hold be elicited and explored so that they can be incorporated into public health decisions and practice? This chapter concentrates on the first topic. The second topic is discussed in Chapter 11, on public participation.

The aim of public health practice is to improve health and decrease disease in the population. However, as we have seen in other chapters, policy decisions are not made only using the criterion of whether they will produce maximum health gain for a given resource, but also take into account other ethical considerations, such as whether they are fair (the principle of justice), whether they infringe people's right to choose for themselves what is in their own best interest (the principle of autonomy) or whether they may do significant harm to a minority (the principle of non-maleficence). These principles offer a starting point to plan research activity in public health medicine.

Although bioethical principles are useful as an abstract reference against which to judge our practice (prima facie principles), in each situation applying the different principles can lead to different conclusions about the most appropriate course of action. There is no one bioethical principle or theory that is universally accepted as overriding. Most people use a mixture of ethical approaches in different situations. When these approaches produce conflicting conclusions about the morally correct course of action, people do not consistently give priority to the same bioethical principle when resolving the conflict. For example, some argue for the compulsory fluoridation of water in the UK because it would bring a large health gain at minimal risk, despite the fact that such a course of action would infringe the autonomy of a significant number of people. At the same time, they oppose compulsory vaccination in the UK because it infringes autonomy, despite the fact that it would produce health gain at minimal risk.

Key considerations leading to these different, apparently inconsistent, positions might include: the degree of benefit from the proposed intervention; the number of people and the extent to which they support or object to the proposed intervention; the feasibility and consequences of alternative courses of action (such as, say, only fluoridating the water of those who give informed consent versus only vaccinating those who give informed consent); and the nature of potential harm involved (e.g. a small risk shared evenly across the population versus a low probability risk that might significantly harm a minority). To resolve the moral dilemmas in such situations, different ethical principles need to be traded off against each other according to the degree to which they are threatened or supported.

Given the fact that most people employ a plurality of ethical approaches to inform or justify their decisions, and that in some situations there is the possibility of conflicts between the different principles, it is not possible to define in advance a system of rules of behaviour for governing the conduct of research or the practice of public health. Since no algorithm can be applied to determine *a priori* what is ethical, we need to develop processes that enable us to examine the ethical aspects of our practice. Public participation, discussed in Chapter 11, is one process that can help. Another is to develop methods for ethical reflection. This chapter proposes one way of examining the ethical implications of public health research. It considers the key aspects of different study designs and the implications these have for each of the main bioethical principles. This approach produces a multidimensional matrix that allows us to identify study designs in which different ethical theories may compete with each other or where certain bioethical principles are particularly threatened. Such a matrix can act as a guide to the areas which are important to consider when reflecting on the ethics of a particular piece of public health research. In summary, one needs to consider the nature of research being conducted, as well as ethical principles in order to decide whether it is morally justified.

The ethics of research in general

What is research?

Research can be defined as the construction of generalisable knowledge and is distinguished from *investigation* which generates information but not knowledge, and *technology* which is the applied use of knowledge. There are many different study designs that can be used to construct the knowledge needed for public health practice. The choice of study design will depend both on the type of question being asked (e.g. What caused this disease? What is the prognosis of this condition? Is this intervention effective?) and on bioethical considerations. It is not always ethically desirable to choose the method that, from an epistemological perspective, provides the most reliable information. In other words, certain study designs may offer high quality information but only at the expense of violating bioethical principles.

General ethical principles of research

There are many well-established codes of practice that cover the ethics of research. Some of the widely accepted principles include:

- Research should be methodologically sound: it should have a design that is capable of testing the hypothesis being investigated; it should be of sufficient size to have the power to produce an answer.
- The study should be conducted appropriately and data analysed in an unbiased way.
- Findings should be presented honestly: investigators should not fabricate data or distort their results.
- Plagiarism and failure to acknowledge the contributions of others is unethical.
- Investigators should not suppress unwanted findings (there is ongoing debate about the extent to which and the timescale within which people should share their results).
- Investigators should declare conflicts of interest.

It goes without saying that all the ethical principles that apply to research in general also apply to public health research. This chapter will therefore concentrate on the ethical issues that arise because of the specific nature of public health research, which has human beings (particularly groups of people) for its subject matter and involves balancing the needs and interests of individuals against the needs and interests of other individuals, or the needs of society in general.

Hidden values of research

Researchers should be aware that the choice of research question, the outcomes measured and the population on which the research is to be conducted all are value-laden decisions. It is not possible for researchers to be completely objective; therefore it is important for investigators to try to identify their own perspective and values and to try and incorporate the perspectives and values of the population being researched. Oliver has looked at the outcomes used in several randomised control trials (RCTs) looking at the effectiveness of epidural anaesthesia in labour.[1] Many outcomes are measured, including perinatal death rate and measures of fetal hypoxia (neonatal blood pH). She also looks at the outcomes used in several RCTs looking at the effectiveness of having social support during labour. Many of the same outcomes as the first trial, such as perinatal mortality, are looked at but the trials do not record neonatal blood pH. They also look at additional outcomes such the relationship between mother and baby (e.g. breast feeding at 3 months), not considered in the epidural trials. She asks, why is the quality of the mother–child relationship not measured in epidural trials? Is it not important to know if this intervention interferes with bonding? And why is neonatal blood pH not measured in the trials looking at social support? Is it not important to know if this intervention may make the child more hypoxic? Both questions are important to the mother and child. Oliver's conclusion is that the trials are designed by anaesthetists and midwives, respectively, to answer their own questions. Patient participation in the study design might have made the findings more relevant to the participants and thus more ethical.

Bioethical principles and the choice of study design

Epidemiology

The basic science underlying public health is epidemiology. However, public health is a multidisciplinary activity and research from many disciplines, such as the social sciences, psychology, medicine or economics, among other fields, will inform its practice. This chapter focuses on epidemiological research, although most of the ethical considerations are equally applicable to other disciplines relevant to public health.

Epidemiology is the study of the distribution, frequency and determinants of health and disease in human populations. The purpose of epidemiology is to obtain, interpret and use health information to promote health and reduce disease. Epidemiology is not just concerned with death, illness and disability, but also with positive health states and the means to improve health. It is not only interested in treatments and health programmes but also considers the socio-economic determinants of ill-health.

Epidemiological studies can be used to *describe* the health of groups of people, to *explain* patterns of health and disease, to *plan* interventions to improve health or prevent harm and to *evaluate* interventions and health services.

Epidemiological studies have various designs. The key elements of epidemiological study designs that will be used to examine the implications for bioethical theories are:

- the purpose of the study;
- whether the study is experimental or observational;
- the state of health of the people or populations being studied;
- the unit of study: individuals; groups; populations;
- the time axis: is it a prospective or retrospective study?

The main bioethical principles that they will be considered in relation to are:

- respect for people (this includes the principle of autonomy (respecting an individual's right to self-determination) and the principle of protecting the vulnerable (e.g. people who are mentally incompetent, minors, prisoners, etc.);
- justice;
- beneficence;
- non-maleficence.

AMANDA BURLS, JUAN CABELLO-LÓPEZ

The purpose of the study: to protect people or generate knowledge?

All the ethical principles that guide public health practice apply to public health research. However, since the primary purpose of research is to generate knowledge, not to prevent harm or protect health, public health research is not justified by the principle of beneficence to the same degree as public health practice. Consequently, it is especially incumbent on investigators to ensure that subjects are protected from harm (non-maleficence). Human research is, therefore, subject to more stringent ethical criteria than other health activity, to protect subjects from research risks. This principle is encapsulated in the section on non-clinical research in the Declaration of Helsinki which states 'In research on man, the interest of science and society should never take precedence over considerations related to the well-being of the subject.'[2]

Safeguards to protect research subjects, such as the review of research proposals by ethics committees or review boards, are commonplace. However, it is not always straightforward to distinguish public health practice from public health research: both use the same scientific methodology; both can generate generalisable knowledge. Public health activities like surveillance,[3] responding to emergencies (e.g. investigating an outbreak of Legionnaires' Disease) and programme evaluation (e.g. an audit of cervical screening reports) are examples of activities that border on research. How can we decide which activities should be submitted for formal ethical review? The US Center for Disease Control and Prevention[4] classifies activity by its primary intent: if the primary intent of a project or study is to prevent injury or control disease, the project is non-research; if the primary intent is to generate generalisable knowledge, the project is research.

Experimental versus observational study design

Observational studies are studies that observe and measure factors affecting different individuals, groups or populations, while experimental studies involve deliberately producing a change in some factor to observe its effect on individuals, groups or populations.

Observational studies

The majority of epidemiological studies are observational. Observational studies are much less likely to threaten the principle of non-maleficence than experimental studies, since they carry minimal risk to those involved. The risk of harm tends to come mainly from the poor conduct of a study leading to, say, invasion of privacy or breach of confidentiality. There may also be disbenefits or harm from examinations or tests. However, if observational studies involve asking questions, carrying out examinations or tests, then the nature, size and justification of any potential risk should be considered and informed consent is required to protect the right to self-determination (autonomy).

Experimental studies

Since experimental studies involve intervening in the world, ethical principles that deal with the consequences of actions, such as the principles of non-maleficence, beneficence and justice, need particular attention. Careful assessment of potential risk and possible benefit needs to be carried out to protect the subject and ensure that the problem being addressed justifies the extent of any risk being undertaken. The potential threat to participants' autonomy in experimental clinical studies is dealt with by the requirement of informed consent. Recently the importance of selecting subjects to avoid inequity on the basis of age, socio-economic status or other variables has been recognised. This ensures that everyone who has the potential to benefit from a treatment has an equal chance of being recruited, that findings are generalisable to all groups who might benefit, and that the risk of exploitation of certain groups within society, e.g. the socio-economically disadvantaged, is minimised.

The principles of beneficence and non-maleficence have led to the notion of 'equipoise' as an ethical requirement of a clinical trial. Being in equipoise means that investigators (or at least the scientific collective) must be in balanced doubt about the likely usefulness of the intervention being examined.[5] If people are not in equipoise, then, either a treatment that, on the balance of probabilities, is believed to be beneficial is being withheld from a patient or group, or a patient or group is being exposed to a treatment that, on the balance of probabilities, is believed to be harmful. Since researchers are rarely neutral in their assessment about the probability that a treatment will be useful (investigators tend to be motivated to do trials on interventions they think will be helpful), there has been much debate about how much doubt constitutes 'equipoise'. Some take a strict view and think that there should be a genuine belief in the equal probability of either outcome, others argue that we are in equipoise unless the research evidence is 'beyond reasonable doubt' (conventionally, p < 0.05). Empirical studies suggest that half of clinicians think that equipoise is disturbed to the point of making a trial unethical beyond a 70 : 30 balance.[6]

In an observational study there is no need for researchers to be in equipoise about the possible benefits or disbenefits of the exposure under investigation. For example, epidemiologists can investigate concerns that sleeping position may predispose the child to sudden infant death syndrome (SIDS) without being in equipoise about whether it does or not, provided they examine this hypothesis with an observational study such as a case-control study.[7]

Distinguishing between study designs

It is important to truly distinguish between observational and experimental study designs. This is not always straightforward; what starts as an observational study may evolve into an experimental study. If this goes by unnoticed, ethical conflicts can be overlooked. A notorious example is the Tuskegee syphilis experiment in the United States.[8] The study was set up to investigate the natural history of untreated syphilis in black men. Questions about the prognosis or natural history of a disease are best answered by prospective cohort studies.[9] Thus the epistemologically best design to answer this question would be to take a group of people with syphilis who are not going to be treated and follow them to see what happens to them compared to what happens to a similar group without syphilis or with treated syphilis. Most readers will probably reject such a study design as unethical because it involves withholding an effective treatment from a group of patients who would benefit from it. Nonetheless this study was carried out in the US on 399 black men with syphilis from one of the poorest counties in Alabama. Given that there is no right to health care in the USA (see Chapter 5 by Locock, 'International perspectives on priority-setting in health care') and that millions of American citizens have no access to health care and no health care insurance, it is at least theoretically possible to argue (as the investigators did) that there was no moral obligation to treat the research subjects. Even if the argument that within the context of the US medical system such an action is not unethical *per se* were granted, surely the participants had the right to know the nature of the infection they have? This would seem to be required by the concept of autonomy and respect for the individual which is the very ethical principle used to justify the grossly unequal distribution of access to health care in the US. These men were simply told that they had 'bad blood'. Researchers went even further: they ensured that the men who registered for the draft were exempted from military service so that they would not undergo a medical examination and inadvertently get treated for their syphilis. Thus an ethically questionable observational study became converted to an entirely morally indefensible experiment whose primary objective, knowledge, was obtainable only by violating the principles of non-maleficence, autonomy and justice. By the end of the experiment, which was halted in 1972, 28 men had died directly from syphilis, 100 had died from complications of syphilis, 40 wives had been infected and 19 children had been born with congenital syphilis.

The unit of study

Implications for experimental designs

The ethics of experimental research on human subjects has been widely discussed and there is widespread agreement, consolidated into codes of practice, declarations and guidelines as to how this research should be conducted to protect the individual. The Nuremberg Code[10] stresses such principles as: voluntary informed consent (that can be withdrawn at any time); the avoidance of all unnecessary physical and mental suffering; the degree of risk should be in proportion to humanitarian importance of the problem. The Declaration of Helsinki (IV) has twelve basic principles covering similar areas as the Nuremberg Code, but also dealing with the quality of research design, conduct, dissemination and consent when the subject is a minor or his or her physical or mental incapacity makes it impossible to obtain informed consent directly.

Most debate and consensus, however, has focused on clinical trials on individuals. However, in public health the unit of study is not usually the individual but groups and populations. This can have important ethical implications for the conduct of a study. For example, in some intervention studies aimed at groups or populations (e.g. a media campaign testing the best advertising strategy to increase the use of condoms) it is not possible to get the informed consent of the individuals.[11] Informed consent in such cases should be sought from a proxy or agent for the population, such as an ethics committee, community leaders, politicians (preferably from a number of representative sources). Since informed consent of individuals is not possible and they do not have the option of withdrawing from the study, the principle of autonomy is violated. It is important that the importance and degree of this should be assessed and weighed against potential benefits.

Another issue that arises from the unit of study being groups or populations is that the benefits and harms may not fall equally on everyone within the population. Sometimes the rights and interests of some people have to be balanced against the rights and interests of others.

Implications for observational study designs

It is established practice that people who are the subjects of research should have given their informed consent to participate in the research. However, epidemiological studies often use routinely collected data that has not been collected expressly for the purpose of research. This can potentially threaten the principle of autonomy because it is not logistically possible to get informed consent from everyone whose information is included. It can also pose a threat to people's privacy.[12] Solutions include:

- anonymisation of data so that information cannot be linked to the individual;
- aggregation of data;
- routine notification to patients that data collected for clinical purposes may be used for research with the opportunity for the patient to opt out.

It is important to conduct research properly so that both the threat to privacy by research and the threat to research by maintaining privacy are minimised.

The state of health of the people or populations being studied

The ethics of a particular study design may depend on whether the participants are healthy or ill. If a patient is ill and seeks help, a health professional may provide treatment (or investigate treatments) whose effectiveness is uncertain, in the hope of directly benefiting the individual. However if health professionals approach healthy people and offer them health promotion interventions (e.g. vaccination or screening) or ask them to become involved in research, any individual benefit is at best indirect and deferred. It is, therefore, even more essential that there is convincing evidence that the risk of harm from research is minimal when subjects are healthy.

In this context it is also important to consider the ethical implications of doing research on people who are physically or mentally incompetent. Where research subjects are able to give informed consent, they may often be willing to accept some risks simply for altruistic reasons. Thus healthy volunteers will often participate in research which causes discomfort or carries some small risk. People who are not able to give informed consent should not be the subjects of research unless both informed consent has been received on their behalf from an appropriate person or body (e.g. a court) *and* there is the possibility of direct benefit to them.

Sometimes different bioethical principles will compete. Recently a proposal for a multicentre randomised controlled trial involving elderly patients in the UK had to go before several local ethics committees. Conflicting judgements were made about whether patients with cognitive impairment should be included. Some committees approved the trial provided such patients *were not included* as they were unable to give informed consent. Other committees approved the trial only on the condition that such patients *were included* so that they had the opportunity to benefit and results would be generalisable and would not discriminate against cognitively impaired patients.

Time axis

Whether a study is prospective or retrospective affects the degree to which it could potentially violate different bioethical principles. For example, in a retrospective study the principles of non-maleficence and beneficence are relatively unthreatened, because no changes are being brought about. Exceptionally, a poorly conducted study may lead to harm if there were, for example, a breach of confidentiality.

Prospective studies have more potential for unwanted effects. It is impossible to observe without affecting the system observed. Thus prospective studies are more likely to produce unintended outcomes than retrospective studies. (Sometimes it may become ethically imperative to intervene as a consequence of what is observed or discovered.) This means that we must try to anticipate potential effects of prospective studies and ensure that the principles governing the consequences of actions (non-maleficence, beneficence and justice)

145

are not at risk of being violated. As noted above, experimental studies are much more vulnerable than observational prospective studies in this respect.

Conclusion

By being aware of the possible threats to bioethical principles posed by different aspects of epidemiological study designs, researchers can consciously address the ethical implications of a proposed study and anticipate, avoid or resolve possible ethical problems. This process of active ethical reflection is aimed at improving our decision-making but it is not a cookbook and it should be recognised that

> Different conclusions may result from different ethical reviews of the same issue or proposal, and each conclusion may be ethically reached, given varying circumstances of place and time; a conclusion is ethical not merely because of what has been decided but also owing to the process of conscientious reflection and assessment by which it has been reached.[13]

Notes

1 S. Oliver, 'Lay perspectives on questions of effectiveness', in A. Maynard and I. Chalmers, eds, *Non-random Reflections on Health Services Research*, London: British Medical Journal Publishing Group, 1997, pp. 272–91.
2 World Medical Association, Declaration of Helsinki (IV), 1949; amended 1989.
3 Surveillance is the ongoing, systematic collection, analysis, interpretation and timely dissemination of outcome-specific data for the purpose of prevention and controlling injury or disease, e.g. monitoring congenital birth defects. See S. B. Thacker and R. L. Berkelman, 'Public health surveillance in the United States', *Epidemiologic Review* 10 (1988), pp. 164–90.
4 Dixie E. Snider, Guidelines for defining public health research and public health non-research, an electronic article produced by the Center for Disease Control and Prevention, Atlanta, Ga.
5 J. Neuberger, 'The patient's view of the patient–health care worker relationship', in R. Gillon, ed., *Principles of Health Care Ethics*, London: John Wiley, 1994, pp. 377–86.
6 N. Johnson, R. J. Lilford, W. Brazier, 'At what level of collective equipoise does a clinical trial become ethical?', *Journal of Medical Ethics* 17 (1991), pp. 30–4.

RESEARCH METHODS IN PUBLIC HEALTH

7 Case-control studies are observational studies in which groups of people who have a disease or other outcome of interest are compared to a control group who are similar but do not have the outcome, to see if there are risk factors or exposures that are associated more often with one group than the other.

8 J. H. Jones, *Bad Blood: The Tuskegee Syphilis Experiment*, New York: Free Press, 1993.

9 Cohort studies are observational studies that compare a group of people with an exposure or risk factor to a comparison (or 'control') group that do not have this exposure and follow them up to see whether there are different outcomes associated with each group.

10 Trials of war criminals before the Nuremberg Military Tribunals under Control Council Law No. 10, 181–2, 1949. Washington DC: US Government Printing Office, 1949.

11 S. J. L. Edwards, D. A. Braunholtz, R. J. Lilford and A. J. Stevens, 'Ethical issues in the design and conduct of cluster randomised controlled trials', *British Medical Journal* 318 (1999), pp. 1407–9.

12 T. Ackerman, 'Medical research, society and health care ethics', in Gillon, *Principles of Health Care Ethics*, pp. 874–83.

13 Council for International Organizations of Medical Sciences, *International Guidelines for Ethical Review of Epidemiological Studies*, Geneva: CIOMS, 1991.

11

PUBLIC PARTICIPATION IN PUBLIC HEALTH DECISIONS

Amanda Burls

Introduction

Public health care is concerned with the health of populations. Public health practitioners take a wider view than health care practitioners, whose primary responsibility is to help individual patients. Thus while doctors or nurses are usually concerned to deliver the best possible care to the patients they are treating, public health specialists will step back from this direct interaction and may be concerned about the people who do not use or have access to health services. Also, they might wonder whether there is some intervention that could have prevented the ill-health in the first place. The responsibilities of public health practitioners vary from place to place but can include roles such as developing health promotion strategies, protection from and investigation of environmental hazards, communicable disease control, vaccination programmes, health care needs assessment, community development and the evaluation and planning of health services. The common theme behind all these tasks is that decisions are being made about and on behalf of groups of people, not individuals.

Since the aim of public health practice is to promote health and prevent disease, its activity is firmly based on the principle of beneficence (doing good). Many public health practitioners take it for granted that, since their role is to work on behalf of populations to produce maximum health gain, utilitarian principles (the greatest good for the greatest number) provide the fundamental ethical framework to guide their decisions. However, the principle of justice is also important. The NHS, for example, is founded upon the principle of universal access even though this is not necessarily the most efficient form of delivering care. One might, for example, be able to achieve more health gain for a fixed sum of money by providing extra health services in urban areas and none in rural areas, but may not choose to do this because it would not be 'fair'. So, how can we ensure that public health practice is ethically sound? We have seen from other chapters that it is not possible to select one ethical framework and apply it to all problems to crank out the solution to the question of what is the most ethical course of action. Each decision is different and must be considered in the light of all the ethical principles we accept. Codes of practice and checklists may guide us but they are not a substitute for ethical reflection. In the absence of ethical theories or frameworks that can simply be applied to problems, one solution is to focus on the *process* or *processes* of making decisions. Elements of such processes that can help us make more ethical decisions include veracity, explicitness, openness, accountability, and explicit ethical reflection. This chapter considers the role of public involvement in decision-making as a means of facilitating ethical practice and resolving ethical dilemmas.

Public participation in health care decisions

In clinical practice there has been a shift in the perception of the doctor–patient relationship. Traditionally the physician had a paternal role, making decisions about what he thought was in the best interests of his patient; and patients were expected to accept treatment or advice without question. Our society no longer considers this to be the most appropriate model for the ideal doctor–patient relationship and there has been a gradual shift to more patient participation. The degree of involvement covers a whole spectrum from simply giving patients more information, through listening to their priorities, through to a partnership model of practitioner–patient relationship with shared decision-making. This latter is often advocated today as the ideal but is seen less in practice than in theory. The change in patient–practitioner relationships is reflected in the growing emphasis on the principle of autonomy (the idea that people should be able to reflect on their own best interests and make decisions for themselves). In the USA with its more individualistic, market-based, philosophy, the principle of autonomy is sometimes taken still further with the patient assuming the role of the informed consumer and the doctor playing a subordinate role as purveyor of medical expertise and information; the ultimate decisions are made by the consumer.

Whatever the particular model of practitioner–patient interaction, practitioners have always been constrained by the principles of non-maleficence and beneficence, i.e. the avoidance of inflicting evil or harm and the promotion of good or health. Thus the patient's interest have always been the central dynamic behind decisions, whether this interest has been interpreted by the doctor or by the patient.

Analogously, public health practitioners have always worked to improve the health of and prevent harm to the populations for which they are responsible. Just as with clinical medicine, public health practitioners have traditionally acted upon their own interpretations of what is in the public interest and have not questioned whether this is, in fact, what the public want. Often decisions have been made behind closed doors with little information being made available to the general public. Explicitness and openness have not traditionally been hallmarks of policy decisions in the UK. There are numerous health policy decisions made implicitly every year. These decisions include: which screening programmes are available to the public; which vaccines are available to the population to combat infectious disease; and whether or not to accept genetically modified food on supermarket shelves.

There has been more and more empirical evidence accumulating to show that politicians, doctors, nurses and policy-makers have different priorities from the public and from each other. The question is, whose values should count? My personal view, as a public health doctor, is that, as we work on behalf of the population, our decisions should reflect the values and interests of the people we serve. Since our preconceptions of what these values and interests are differ from the reality, we need to be able to elicit and explore the public's opinion. One way to do this is to increase public participation in decision-making. The rest of this chapter considers different ways of involving the public and concludes with a reflection on the ethical problems that these processes can also bring.

Public participation in health policy decisions

The first rung on the ladder: information

Just as the first step towards patients becoming involved in decisions affecting their own health care is the availability of good quality, accessible information, so the lowest level of public involvement in public health policy is the provision of information. Information about policy decisions is gradually becoming more available to the public with, for example, publication of annual reports by the Director of Public Health for each health authority and the increasing tendency to publish discussion and strategy documents. Some health authorities now permit members of the public to observe their board meetings (provided subjects that would otherwise breach patient confidentiality are not being discussed). Many health authorities have also set up websites to inform the public (although these contain little detail as yet). Despite this slow shift to more openness, the penetration of information to members of the public is negligible. For the public to be involved in health policy decision-making it needs to be given access to high quality information about health so that it may join in a democratic process.

The failure of public authorities to give the public information in an adequate form is more starkly shown in the public health scares of the 1990s in the UK, for example the link between BSE and new variant Creutzfeld Jakob Disease, and the oral contraceptive pill and venous thrombosis. In the former case, the risk was understated by public authorities who equated unknown risk (i.e. no evidence that there was risk) with no risk to health. In the latter case, the risk was exaggerated and led to many unwanted pregnancies. If risk is not appropriately communicated, it is not possible to make informed decisions.

Public participation through democracy

Personal health

There are many levels at which the public can participate in health care decisions. The most basic is when people participate in the decisions about their own care (or the care of family members). However, these decisions are constrained by the treatments available because of implicit or explicit policy decisions, and have negligible, if any, influence on future policy decisions.

National influence

The most indirect but most fundamental level at which the public can influence policy is during elections, when it can vote for a government with a particular health care philosophy, which will set

the budget that ultimately affects the extent of health care that can
be provided. This is a blunt instrument for public participation:
there is usually only the opportunity to vote every four or five
years with a very limited range of choice; there is little information
about what is really going on; and there are competing issues
which could affect the decision for whom to vote.

Local democracy

In England, there is no direct democratic input into or accountability of health authorities. These are appointed bodies and are
responsible to the Secretary of State for Health. Public participation
could be increased if health authorities were accountable to locally
elected representatives, or if the public was allowed a democratic
vote about the appointment of the members of the board or the
chairperson, etc.

Identifying public values through research

Recently there has been a surge of research into the public's values.
Much of this has been done by economists who are keen to know the
utility that people attach to different health states and treatments, in
order to help prioritise health care interventions. There are many
new techniques that are being developed to elicit people's views
and include both qualitative and quantitative research methods.
The information provided by this sort of research can be used by
the public health practitioner to help inform the decisions he or
she makes as the citizen's agent. However, much of this work is
still embryonic, with experimental methodologies that are yet to
be validated. Caution must be used when interpreting such research
evidence. Important questions to bear in mind are:

- How were the participants of the research selected?
- Are they likely to be representative of the general population?
- Is there a large class or ethnic bias in those chosen or willing to
  participate in such research?
- Are they professional representatives of the public (such as
  members of patient support groups), random citizens or patients
  or their carers? (We know that these different groups have
  different interests and values.)

Participation on particular decisions

There are many ways in which the public can participate in particular policy decisions. Sometimes the government or health authorities will undertake a public consultation process, in which members of the public can give their views at public meetings or in writing. Sometimes special groups are set up to consider topics in depth and public and patient representatives are invited to join. (All the questions above, about the representativeness of these individuals and how they are selected, will apply in these situations as well.) Several chapters in this book give examples of how 'representative' members of the public were involved in priority-setting decisions, particularly in relation to funding extra-contractual referrals (ECRs). There is no reason why such models could not be adapted for resolving other health policy questions, such as whether water should be fluoridated to prevent dental decay.

Citizens' juries

A much bolder and fuller form of public participation is the citizen's jury. (An example of where a citizens' jury was used by a health authority is given in Chapter 4, by Needham.) A citizen is a person who has a public interest in the social policies being made, i.e. an interest over and above his or her own particular interest in the decision under discussion. A citizens' jury brings together a group of citizens to consider the issue in a neutral and impartial way, informed by the best evidence available. The jury, after due consideration, gives its recommendations which may or may not be binding, depending on how the jury was constituted.

These juries represent public participation at its most developed level but are expensive and time consuming and cannot be used for all decisions. They are perhaps best used to establish overall policy, and 'case law' where issues are controversial.

Very few citizens' juries are set up so that their recommendations are binding and this has led to some people expressing scepticism about their real role. They suggest that the juries are used to give a pseudo-legitimacy to controversial decisions in cases where their recommendations agree with those of the authorities, and that they are quietly ignored when their conclusions are unwelcome.

AMANDA BURLS

Training and support

It can be quite intimidating for lay people to sit in with professionals in order to participate in joint decision-making. Often public representatives on such groups will either say nothing or will be 'professional' patients and not truly representative. One way of helping 'ordinary' members of the public effectively communicate and get their viewpoint over is to give them support and help them develop skills and confidence to operate in such groups. In the UK the 'Voices' project has tried to do just that and has had considerable success. The Critical Appraisal Skills Programme (CASP) has worked with consumers and multidisciplinary groups to help people develop the skills to make sense of scientific evidence. As one lay member of a multidisciplinary group that advises the health authority on the provision of health services commented, 'I wanted to be on this committee because I felt I had things I wanted to say; after the CASP training I now feel I have a voice.'

Challenging decisions

Public health practitioners continually make decisions. It would be impossible for the public to participate in every one of them. Ideally, therefore, there should exist some mechanisms whereby the public can question decisions. In many places the only avenue for challenging health policy decisions is through the law courts. This is not a realistic method for most people. Some health authorities that are trying to develop objective ethical frameworks for making prioritising decisions are beginning to think about processes whereby the public can appeal against decisions (see Chapter 3, by Griffiths). Often there are established complaints procedures and Community Health Councils (CHCs) will also act as patient advocates; but these have little power or influence. It would greatly enable the public to participate in health policy decisions if there were user-friendly channels where they could voice their opinions and be listened to in a constructive, non-confrontational environment.

Other considerations

We have seen how public participation can take many different forms. As argued at the start of this chapter my personal view is that public participation 'is a good thing', and can help ensure

154

that decisions are ethical, helping people to know what really is in the best interests of the community they serve and opening up procedures to reflection and accountability. However, involving the public can bring its own ethical problems.

What if the public is wrong?

We have seen that the public's values do not always agree with those of the professionals (empirical examples are given in Part I). Often public health professionals are quite willing to accept the public's values and interests and work towards achieving these even when these values conflict with their own opinion, much as a surgeon will respect a patient's decision not to be operated on even though he or she thinks it is in the patient's best interest. However, what if we truly believe that the public is wrong? Whose values should we use? Should we really not treat patients with HIV because prejudice and negative stereotyping means that the public gives a higher priority to spending the money on stopping children sucking their thumbs? A majority can behave despotically and unfairly towards a minority. Should this be permitted? If not, should it be public health practitioners that set themselves up as the guardians of morality?

Irrational activity

What should we do if the public want irrational or useless activities? Should we fund a service or intervention that has been shown to be clinically ineffective (or even downright harmful) just because the public wants it? Irrational demands from the public are not uncommon. The following is a case study from one Health Authority where I worked.

Local councillors reported a possible cluster of childhood leukaemia to the health authority, who investigated the cluster. Investigations confirmed that there had been five cases of childhood leukaemia in the area over an eight-year period but there was not an excess incidence over the expected rate for childhood leukaemia in the town. It was concluded that the apparent cluster was an illusion due to *post hoc* boundary definitions, a conclusion supported by expert epidemiologists and researchers outside the area. Despite the fact that there was almost certainly no cluster at all, the press and local families and politicians were adamant that there was a cluster and started a campaign demanding that the health authority set up a special enquiry or epidemiological study to investigate what had caused leukaemia in these children. At the time (and still at the time of writing), the cause of childhood leukaemia was not known and there was no epidemiological study design that would have revealed the cause of leukaemia from just five cases with no primary hypothesis. Much larger numbers are required. A multi-million pound study of appropriate design and adequate size was at that time in progress in the UK (the UK Childhood Cancer Study), which had the power to have a chance of providing the answers people wanted. Nonetheless, a 4,000 plus signature petition was handed in to the health authority and to Downing Street demanding a special study. What should the health authority do in this situation? Should it undertake an investigation that was scientifically useless because the population wanted it? This is certainly what many health authorities have done in the past. There are innumerable examples of cluster studies that predictably have been unable to reach a conclusion.

Sadly, these studies are not usually done because the health authorities are committed to acting in accordance with the public demands even if they do not agree with them, but for pragmatic public relations reasons: it is the quickest way to contain public protest and to be perceived as acting in the interests of the population. (It is the population equivalent of giving patients a prescription for antibiotics for a viral sore throat because it is the fastest way to get them out of the surgery and make them happy.) In Northamptonshire the Director of Public Health supported the view that it was unethical (and disrespectful to the families) to carry out a useless investigation as a public relations exercise. Instead, a risk communication exercise was started, involving concerned members of the public, to try to communicate the limitations of epidemiological methods and reassure people that appropriate research was in progress.

What should be done when there is plurality of views amongst the public?

We have already noted that patients and carers may have different interests from the general citizen, but sometimes there may be even more profound differences in values. This can happen because people have fundamentally different ethical theories. For example, some may think individual freedom, or autonomy, is the most important principle while others believe that social solidarity and justice are more important. Such people may have diametrically opposed attitudes to certain health policies such as fluoridation or compulsory vaccination. So those, for example, who think autonomy is the most important principle may argue that, even though they accept that fluoridation of water supplies will produce a large health gain with negligible risk, the practice is nonetheless unethical since there is a minority of individuals who do not accept it and whose autonomy would be infringed. While those who think social justice is most important will point out that the large health gain favours the most deprived groups in the population, and children who have a right to the protection and care of society. This is the 'professional' view expounded by Holt, Real and Breach in Chapter 12, on fluoridation. How can such conflicts be resolved? Should the rights of a minority be allowed to prevent good being done for the majority, even when there is no objective risk to the minority?

What if people do not want to participate in decisions?

There is evidence that many people do not want to participate in decision-making (especially if this entails rationing health care). There are a variety of reasons why people may not want to participate: they feel they do not have the expertise; they do not want to take the responsibility of denying people treatment; they do not wish to spare the time; they think paid professionals should make these decisions; they lack the self-confidence to do so. There is research evidence that suggests that people with a higher educational level and jobs where they already take responsibility for difficult decisions are more willing to participate in decision-making about the prioritisation of health care. People who are relatively disadvantaged or disempowered are less likely to want to be involved. This means that the views given by the public are not necessarily representative. Should people be obliged or encouraged to participate in decisions if they do not want to? There are some precedents: in some societies voting is compulsory; in the UK jury service is a duty that all eligible citizens are expected to fulfil whether they want to or not. Would obligatory participation threaten the principle of autonomy? If people are not obliged to participate, does it matter that the views expressed will under-represent the most disadvantaged in our society?

Conclusion

Public participation in health policy formulation can lead to more ethically acceptable decisions for two main reasons. First, public health decisions are being made on behalf of the population and public participation can help ensure that they more accurately reflect the public's interests and values. Second, public participation helps contribute to an open process that encourages active ethical reflection and provides a strategy for resolving conflicting conclusions from different ethical theories. In order for this to occur, professionals need to give high quality information and have adequate processes to involve the public in decision-making. However, it is not a simple solution and achieving a consensus from a variety of viewpoints can also present ethical dilemmas to the public health practitioner.

12

ETHICAL CONSIDERATIONS IN WATER FLUORIDATION

Ruth Holt, John Beal and Joanna Breach

Introduction

Fluoride occurs naturally in all water supplies at varying concentrations. Water fluoridation may be defined as the adjustment of naturally occurring levels to an optimum within this range for the purposes of prevention of dental decay (dental caries). The level required depends on climate; in temperate countries the required level is most often 1 part per million. The discovery of relatively less dental disease in children living in areas of naturally occurring optimal levels led to the introduction of schemes of artificial fluoridation in 1945.[1] The exact mode of action of fluoride in preventing caries is not fully understood but may include the direct effects of fluoride present in the mouth (topical), and, to a lesser extent, of that absorbed through the body (systemic).

Since fluoridation was first introduced its effectiveness has been investigated in a large number of studies internationally. These studies have used a variety of methodologies. The results show a consistent effect of fluoridation in reducing the amount of caries in the population to levels similar to those seen in naturally fluoridated areas. In children the benefits of water fluoridation have most often been of the order of a 50 per cent reduction in the number of teeth affected by caries. Reductions in adults may be less but the benefits of fluoridation are lifelong.[2] Dental caries is more prevalent and more severe in children from lower social classes, from disadvantaged families and from some minority ethnic groups. Water fluoridation has been shown to be especially effective in reducing these marked inequalities in oral health.[3]

Despite an overall decline in disease, areas with water fluoridation continue to show consistently lower levels of caries.[4] In practical terms water fluoridation has been shown to reduce both the incidence of toothache and the need for tooth extraction. General anaesthesia may be used particularly for extractions in young children with extensive caries, and fluoridation is unique among preventive measures in having been shown to result in a lesser experience of general anaesthesia for dental purposes.[5]

The safety of water fluoridation has been reviewed and endorsed more than once. Attempts to suggest associations between fluoridation and systemic diseases and disorders have never been substantiated.[6]

Fluoridation as mass medication

Those opposed to fluoridation have sometimes based their criticism on the idea that the measure represents 'mass medication' without offering the choice to refuse treatment. This contention has been rejected legally on at least two occasions on the grounds that fluoride, as a naturally occurring component of water and many foods, is not a drug,[7] and, in the UK, that it does not fall within the meaning of the Medicines Act.[8] It has also been questioned whether administration of any preventive agent or regime should be considered strictly as a treatment. Even if fluoridation were to be classified in this way this may not necessarily resolve the apparent dilemma, since, in answer to the criticism, those in favour of fluoridation might also argue (although perhaps more controversially), that they were being denied access to provision of this form of health care.

Current legal position

The implementation of artificial water fluoridation is carried out by water undertakers (either private companies or public bodies). Since 1990 in England these have all been free standing private companies. The opinion of Lord Jauncey, given in 1983, was that although the measure was beneficial and did no harm, because water fluoridation did not add to the wholesomeness of the water supplied it was *ultra vires*, or outside the power of the water companies to implement.[9] The Water (Fluoridation) Act of 1985, later consolidated in the Water Industry Act of 1991, altered this position with the result that water companies are now empowered to provide water fluoridation if they are requested to do so by the local health authority. Health authorities are obliged to publicise their intentions and to make appropriate consultation before requesting fluoridation. Water companies are not, however, placed under any compulsion to fluoridate,[10] and they have conspicuously failed to introduce fluoridation since the Act came into operation, despite repeated attempts by health authorities.[11]

The next section of this chapter is concerned with the ethical issues that surround fluoridation. The discussion is based on the assumption that artificial fluoridation is both effective and safe.

Ethical issues and water fluoridation

A variety of ethical considerations have emerged during the history of water fluoridation. Although they cannot be regarded as independent of each other, for the purposes of this chapter they will be discussed in terms of:

- water fluoridation and beneficence and non-maleficence;
- water fluoridation and autonomy;
- water fluoridation and justice.

Fluoridation, beneficence and non-maleficence

Dentists, like doctors, in addition to a general duty not to do harm (non-maleficence), also have a special duty to do good (beneficence). It is recognised that the two duties may occasionally conflict since fulfilling a duty not to do harm may prevent a beneficial act. For example, not taking a radiograph of a tooth fractured in a recent accident may remove the hazard of radiation but result in failure to provide the appropriate treatment and, potentially, loss of the tooth in consequence. In the case of water fluoridation it may be thought that there is no conflict, since, if the effectiveness and safety of the measure are accepted, water fluoridation provides good and does no harm.

It may even be suggested that, by not providing benefit and by failing to prevent the harm that accrues if the water is not fluoridated, *not* introducing water fluoridation is itself unethical. However there are at least two difficulties in adopting this approach.

First, although the duties of non-maleficence and beneficence are usually clear in relation to individual patients and dentists, it is more problematic whether they both apply in quite the same way in the

161

case of public health measures such as water fluoridation. This is because no one individual can be shown to have a special duty to fluoridate since it is the collective responsibility of a public authority. This authority may be the public health authority, or it may be considered as being the relevant water authority or company to whom the responsibility has been devolved. Such an authority may have a general duty of non-maleficence (as does anyone in the population), but it may not necessarily have the same special duty of beneficence as do individual doctors or dentists. The second difficulty arises because it is usually accepted that a duty 'not to harm' does not extend to 'harming by omission'.

So overall it may be concluded that whilst implementation of water fluoridation is not unethical since it does not infringe the general duty of non-maleficence, non-implementation is also not unethical since there is difficulty in attributing a duty of beneficence, and consideration of the duty of non-maleficence is limited to harmful acts.

Whilst duties of non-maleficence and beneficence are important, they are by no means the sole ethical principles to be considered. Principles of autonomy and of justice may carry the potential to constrain or override other principles.

Water fluoridation and autonomy

At a community level, water fluoridation provides the greatest level of protection against caries for a given sum of money. As dental caries is often a painful condition, in the context of finite resources fluoridation may therefore result in more 'good' than any other measure to prevent decay. In these terms fluoridation may be regarded as the most ethical way to prevent caries. However, in taking account only of the overall good, this approach may take insufficient account of the interests of any particular individual or of any possible harm he or she may suffer in the process. It may, in particular, take little account of the principle of autonomy.

Autonomy has been defined as 'the capacity to think, decide and act, on the basis of such thought and decision freely and without . . . let or hindrance'.[12] In the case of water fluoridation it may be considered as the freedom for adults to choose the type of water they drink for themselves and their children. The principle of autonomy is qualified by the proviso that any action taken does not harm others. It may also be argued, more controversially, that in promoting the principle of autonomy others should not be deprived of possible benefit.

The argument for the principle of autonomy in relation to any form of health care is powerful and this has been one of the most persistent and difficult issues to resolve in relation to water fluoridation. Those opposed to fluoridation argue that this measure would infringe their own autonomy, or right to choose for themselves or their children. In one case, for example, it was suggested by the plaintiff that the measure represented an infringement of parental rights to decide what children should eat or drink.[13] Equally, however, those who wish to have fluoridation introduced could argue that failure to introduce it reduces their autonomy in choosing to have the benefits of fluoridation for themselves and their children.[14]

It seems difficult to choose between the autonomy of those who choose to have fluoridation and those who oppose it. However, there are two facts which may need to be borne in mind. First, the majority of people are willing to accept limitations to their autonomy for the greater good of the community. Second, both effective autonomy and restrictions on it may be more imaginary than real. This is a consequence of constraints and alternatives. Thus people do have some choice as to whether or not to live in a fluoridated area and may use alternatives, such as bottled water as substitutes for drinking water in areas that are fluoridated even though there may be economic and resource constraints in these choices.

An important aspect of autonomy is the need to determine the wishes of the consumer. For choices affecting a population as a whole, the majority opinion may be taken as an expression of that choice. Where studies have been made there is evidence that public opinion supports water fluoridation.[15]

Autonomy may be considered as being a moral right,[16] yet it is not the only one that water fluoridation can be argued to infringe; other moral rights include the right to bodily integrity and the right not to be treated merely as a means to the ends of others. As a safe measure, in terms of consequent physical harm, water fluoridation will not infringe the first of these. However, the right to bodily integrity of the child who develops caries in the absence of water fluoridation is also not infringed, since caries itself does not arise as a violation of bodily integrity by someone else. Either side in the debate may regard themselves or their children as being used merely as a means to the ends of others.

163

Water fluoridation and justice

One major aim in providing health care may be to direct resources so as to minimise inequalities in health as much as possible. A second may be to use health care resources in the most efficient way (in which health gain is greatest for a given cost).

Water fluoridation may be ethically justified on both of these two counts. In relation to the first, water fluoridation is unique amongst measures to prevent dental disease and to promote oral health in that it has the potential to reach all members of a population irrespective of their utilisation of health care services, dietary patterns or oral hygiene practices. Those reached by water fluoridation include the most socio-economically disadvantaged and vulnerable members of society who may suffer disproportionately high levels of dental caries. With few exceptions studies have demonstrated that water fluoridation reduces the very great inequalities seen in dental disease, particularly in areas where levels are high.[17] Thus the distributive justice argument is strongly in favour of water fluoridation.

However, justice may not be concerned solely with the equity of distribution in relation to a particular clinical need but also be a principle that should govern the use of increasingly scarce resources amongst competing areas of need.

Fluoridation and rationing of health care resources

In the past there was little doubt of the cost-effectiveness of water fluoridation. However, the economic case for fluoridation in some areas may have been weakened by the decline in caries. Although reductions in caries resulting from fluoridation have continued these have been reduced in relative and absolute terms. In areas where caries levels are already low, the economic justification for fluoridation may therefore be reduced, particularly if the cost has to be balanced against competing needs and scarce resources. However, the case for fluoridation remains strong in areas where levels of disease are high.[18] It must also be borne in mind that patterns of dental disease continue to change. There is evidence of a halt in the decline in caries in some age groups and of levels increasing in others.[19] Even in areas where fluoridation may not currently be economically justifiable, the same may therefore not necessarily hold true in the future.

Summary

Water fluoridation has been demonstrated to be a safe and effective measure; it is superior to other measures of reducing dental caries in its effectiveness and in the equity of benefits it provides. In ethical terms it fulfils duties of beneficence and of non-maleficence and appears to infringe no legal rights. Whilst the introduction of this measure may infringe the autonomy of those individuals who oppose it, failure to fluoridate may also infringe the rights of those who wish themselves or their children to benefit from it. Its implementation complies with principles of distributive justice. Consideration of these four principles leads to the conclusion that water fluoridation is ethically justified. That the measure is supported by the majority of the population and produces significant health benefits lends strength to this conclusion.

Notes

1 J. J. Murray, A. J. Rugg Gunn and G. N. Jenkins, *Fluorides in Caries Prevention*, 3rd edn, Oxford: Butterworth/Heinemann,1991, pp. 16–17.
2 J. J. Murray, 'Adult dental health in fluoride and non-fluoride areas', *British Dental Journal* 131 (1971), pp. 391–5. J. J. Murray, 'Adult dental health in fluoride and non-fluoride areas, Part 2: Caries experience in each tooth type', *British Dental Journal* 131 (1971), pp. 437–42. D. O'Mullane and H. Whelton, *Oral Health of Irish Adults 1989–1990*, Dublin: The Stationery Office, 1992.
3 C. L. Carmichael, A. J. Rugg Gunn and R. S. Ferrell, 'The relationship between fluoridation, social class and caries experience in 5-year-old children in Newcastle and Northumberland in 1987', *British Dental Journal* 167 (1989), pp. 57–61. C. M. Jones, G. O. Taylor, J. G. Whittle, D. Evans and D. P. Trotter, 'Water fluoridation, tooth decay in 5-year olds and social deprivation measured by the Jarman score: analysis of data from British dental surveys', *British Medical Journal* 315 (1997), pp. 514–17.
4 J. J. Murray *et al.*, *Fluorides in Caries Prevention*, pp. 58–60. D. J. Evans, A. J. Rugg Gunn and E. D. Tabari, 'The effect of 25 years of water fluoridation in Newcastle assessed in four surveys of 5-year-old children over an 18 year period', *British Dental Journal* 178 (1995), pp. 60–4. British Fluoridation Society, *Dental Health Inequalities in the United Kingdom*, Liverpool: BFS, 1997.
5 Evans *et al.*, '25 years of water fluoridation'. A. J. Rugg Gunn, C. L. Carmichael, A. D. French and J. A. Furness, 'Fluoridation in Newcastle and Nothumberland: a clinical study of 5-year-old children', *British Dental Journal* 142 (1977), pp. 395–402. National Alliance for Equity in Health, *Inequalities in Dental Health*, Liverpool: BFS, 1998.
6 Royal College of Physicians, *Fluorides Teeth and Health*, London: Royal College of Physicians, 1976. E. G. Knox, *Fluoridation of*

Water and Cancer: A Review of the Epidemiological Evidence, Report of the DHSS working party, London: HMSO, 1985. World Health Organization, *Fluorides and Oral Health*, WHO Technical Report Series 846, Geneva: WHO, 1994. National Research Council Academy of Science, *Health Effects of Ingested Fluoride*, Washington, DC: National Academy Press, 1993.

7 Mr Justice Kenny, Fluoridation: Judgement of Mr Justice Kenny in the High Court, Dublin, 1963, no. 915P.

8 Lord Jauncey, Opinion of Lord Jauncey, in causa Mrs Catherine McColl against Strathclyde Regional Council, Edinburgh: The Court of Session, 1983.

9 Lord Jauncey, Opinion.

10 Mr Justice Collins, Opinion of Justice Collins in causa Northumbrian Water Limited ex parte Newcastle and North Tyneside Health Authority, High Court of Justice, London, 1998.

11 P. Castle, Editorial: 'The future of the water industry and its implications for water fluoridation', *Community Dental Health* 9 (1992), pp. 323–7.

12 R. Gillon, *Philosophical Medical Ethics*, Published on behalf of the *British Medical Journal* Chichester: John Wiley and Sons, 1986.

13 Mr Justice Kenny, Judgement.

14 J. Harris, *The Ethics of Fluoridation,* London: British Fluoridation Society, 1997.

15 G. B. Hastings, K. Hughes, S. Lawther and R. J. Lowry, 'The role of the public in water fluoridation: public health champions or anti-fluoridation freedom fighters', *British Dental Journal* 184 (1998), pp. 39–41.

16 Gillon, *Philosophical Medical Ethics*.

17 Jones *et al.*, 'Water fluoridation'.

18 R. L. Akehurst and D. J. Sanderson, 'Cost effectiveness in dental health: a review of strategies available for preventing caries', *British Journal of Medical Economics* 7 (1994), pp. 43–54. D. Sanderson, *Water Fluoridation: an Economic Perspective*, York Health Economics Consortium, University of York, 1998.

19 N. B. Pitts and D. J. Evans, 'The dental caries experience of 5-year-old children in the United Kingdom: Surveys co-ordinated by the British Association for the Study of Community Dentistry', *Community Dental Health* 14 (1997), pp. 47–52. N. B. Pitts, D. J. Evans and Z. J. Nugent, 'The dental caries experience of 12-year-old children in the United Kingdom: Surveys co-ordinated by the British Association for the Study of Community Dentistry', *Community Dental Health* 15 (1998), pp. 49–54.

13

SHOULD CHILDHOOD IMMUNISATION BE COMPULSORY?

Peter Bradley

Introduction

Immunisation is offered to all age groups in the UK, but is mainly given to infants and school age children. Such immunisation is not compulsory, in contrast to other countries, such as the United States. The generally high level of immunisation in the UK[1] can be affected by public perception of the risk of side-effects.[2] This chapter discusses whether compulsory vaccination would be acceptable by considering individual cases where parents have failed to give consent or have explicitly refused consent for their children to be immunised. In particular, the rights are considered of: parents to rear their children according to their own standards, the child to receive health care and the community to be protected from vaccine-preventable infectious disease. The conclusion of the chapter is that compulsory vaccination cannot, with few exceptions, be justified in the UK, in view of the high levels of population immunity which currently exist.

Infectious disease used to be the major cause of mortality in the UK. Immunisation and vaccination programmes were designed to protect *individuals* and their *communities* from infectious diseases. These programmes have partially lessened the burden of mortality and morbidity of infectious disease, but the decline in disease rates is probably largely attributable to other factors, for instance improved sanitation. There is, however, some evidence of the success of immunisation programmes, where immunisation has eliminated such diseases as smallpox.[3] Also, when immunisation programmes are disrupted, the rates of disease increase, as happened with diptheria in the USSR.[4]

Individual benefit or benefit for the community?

Individuals will benefit from immunisation, on average, if the chance of developing morbidity or mortality from the disease *before* immunisation, outweighs the chance of developing morbidity or mortality *after* vaccination (including any side-effects of the vaccination). It cannot, however, be guaranteed that a particular individual will benefit.

Communities and individuals will additionally benefit from immunisation programmes if immunisation of enough people in a community leads to an overall reduction in the chance of developing a disease. That is, it is because of a decreased chance of contact with the disease. This notion is referred to as *herd* or *population immunity*. If sufficient numbers of people are immunised the disease may even be eradicated. The rates of immunisation in the UK are currently very high, despite the absence of a compulsory vaccination policy.[1] Even so, they can fall, most commonly in response to public anxiety about the side-effects of vaccination (a very low risk). Epidemiological evidence suggests that if children were not vaccinated, epidemics could ensue.[5] However, the conclusion of the chapter is that compulsory vaccination cannot be justified in the UK at present, in view of the high levels of population immunity which currently exist.

What is the procedure by which consent is usually obtained to immunise a child in the UK?

In the UK, immunisation normally takes place in a health care setting during an individual consultation, when parents or carers accompany their children. Occasionally immunisation takes place in another setting (e.g. a school) and parents entrust their children's safety to professionals. This situation often arises in mass immunisation campaigns or when children are in foster care.

In most health districts, there is a policy on how consent is obtained for immunisation programmes. A written invitation is sent to parents for each individual vaccination and consent is obtained from the parent at each clinic visit. In routine circumstances, a child may not be legally vaccinated until a parent has consented to the procedure.[6] This legal view considers that the parents' rights to decide on behalf of their children override health care workers' duties of care.

In contrast, there are three viewpoints commonly held by health care workers when consent is not obtained from parents to vaccinate their children:

1 Health-care workers are always justified in vaccinating a child, with or without parental consent, if the procedure promotes a child's best interests.
2 Health-care workers cannot vaccinate children if their parents have not consented to procedure.
3 Parental views must usually be acknowledged and respected, but health care workers can act to protect the child's interests in certain circumstances, e.g. where a child's health is in danger, regardless of the level of consent obtained.

In the first case, despite the legal position, health care workers may feel justified in promoting what they see to be the children's interests above their concern to respect parental wishes. However, I will assume that this is an untenable position as most health care workers would not insist on interventions where the benefit to children is small. For example, they would not insist that seemingly healthy children have a vaccination against a rare, mild disease.

In the second view, in the event of any disagreement, health care workers might feel that respecting parents' choices is the most effective way to promote children's health and that compulsory vaccination would prove counter-productive. A single vaccine is unlikely to offer children reasonable protection against all infectious disease. If parents have not co-operated in the decision, they are less likely to comply with subsequent immunisation or health care interventions.

From the third point of view, if there is a risk of significant harm to the child, it may be reasonable to override a parental refusal. For example, a child in the early stages of rabies can be protected, by immunisation, from almost certain death.[7] The health care worker's statutory and moral duty is then to ensure that the child receives the vaccination, no matter what the parental views, since the child's life is at stake.[8] This is also the case if no answer from the parent can be obtained.

In less extreme circumstances, health care workers might instead consider that their professional duty requires them to listen to and comply with parents' views when they are available, so that they are informed enough to help each child if his or her health subsequently falls below a certain standard, even if this help involves acting against parental wishes.

Vaccination against parental wishes may not be justified, if the benefit to the child is insignificant, because of the risk of wronging parents; specifically, the wrong would be the loss of the parents' right to choose health care for their children. Health care workers need to judge whether interventions benefit children sufficiently to justify acting against the parents' wishes.

Can a rights-based approach resolve the dilemma of whether to have compulsory childhood vaccination?

The rights which are relevant to deciding whether vaccination should be compulsory are: children's rights to health care, parents' rights to raise their children according to their own standards and the right of the community to be protected from preventable infectious disease.

How might rights be defined?

Moral rights are often appealed to as eternal and universal verities although their source is often felt to be obscure.[9] Rights are sometimes seen to promote selfish action as they are viewed to be the concerns of individuals. However, rights can also protect individuals from being exploited by defining the limits of acceptable behaviour in the community.

The communitarian notion of a right implies that the community has some common moral ground. From this common moral ground, the community can agree that in certain circumstances some actions between agents should be compulsory or outlawed. Hart says 'The concept of a right belongs to that branch of morality which is specifically concerned to determine when one person's freedom may be limited by another's'.[10] Mill points out that rights also have corresponding duties.[11]

The problem with these definitions is that a parent and child could hold conflicting rights. A solution to this problem is to consider that rights are *not* necessarily absolute and that, often, in the case of conflicting rights, one right can be considered overriding.

What are the rights and duties of parents?

A generally accepted idea is that the parental right to rear is based on a duty of parents to care for their children to an acceptable level. If they fail to care for their children, they relinquish the right to rear. It is felt that a child has a right to be cared for and this includes a right to receive life-saving vaccination when the child already has an easily curable condition, no matter what the parental view is.

Several writers state that generally in law the presumption is that parents will make good choices for their children.[12] Others explain that parents have to bear the emotional and financial consequences resulting from health care intervention. However, yet other writers point out that the children bear the direct consequences of health care, not their parents. This means parents may not be morally free to make all choices for their children if this acts against the children's interests as perceived by society.

In contrast, some people say that parents have a right to raise their children according to their own standards without interference. There are several arguments to support this view; we shall consider the most persuasive ones.

First, it is argued that parents are entitled to rear their own children because they are genetically related to them or because the mothers declared an interest in the children by bearing them. This may mean that parents are best suited to bond with their children and give them the best care. Unfortunately the bonding process is not inevitable between a parent and a child. Sometimes another carer may form a more suitable relationship with the child. Although genetic relationship is seen as important in our society, it is not automatically enough to entitle a parent to raise his or her child.[13]

Second, families are seen as valuable social institutions, which provide emotional security, foster intimacy and familiarity between their members. It is believed that the family needs to be free from interference to fulfil these roles. This means the family may have a right to privacy.

The right to privacy is derived from the claim that families are intimate entities.[14] However, Archard suggests that the family relationship is not intimate in the same manner as, for example, a sexual relationship in which a third party's interference will prevent the development of the relationship.[15] If a parent is asked to attend an immunisation for his or her child, so that the child's health can be protected, this does not necessarily prove detrimental to the fostering of family relationships.

Archard suggests that the person who has a right to care for the child earns this right by caring for the child. I make the assumption that most people expect the parent or guardian to provide food, shelter and nurture for the child if able to do so. Nurture includes parental duties to maintain a child's health to a *reasonable* level by accessing available health care.

Our definition of maintaining a reasonable standard of health includes protection against major illnesses but not necessarily against minor problems. These, although considered significant by some professionals, would not directly harm the child's health. An example is having crooked teeth. It is difficult to decide into which category an immunisation might fit. It seems that classification would depend on the balance of benefits and risks to the child. For example, the child in the early stages of rabies should be protected by immunisation no matter what the circumstances. But parents who do not want their infants to receive pertussis vaccination are subjecting them to a smaller health risk. On their side of the argument is the risk – though a very small one – that the infant will be harmed by the vaccination, that is, the vaccination might confer long-term brain damage.

The obligation that parents have to maintain a reasonable level of health in a child does not entail a duty to optimise the child's interests. The competing interests of their other children and of the parents themselves stand in the way of such an obligation.[16]

However, a minimum level of care from parents is morally required and they relinquish their right to rear if they fail in this.[17] So children's right to basic care can sometimes override the parents' right to choose, and it is up to health care workers to bear this in mind. We shall return to this point later.

What rights does the community have?

Another potential 'right' needs to be considered before it can be decided whether compulsory vaccination is an acceptable policy in the UK. It is the right of every individual in the community to be protected from infectious disease, by insisting on high levels of childhood vaccination. The grounds for such a right would be that unimmunised children pose a greater risk of infection to the community than immunised children.

It is difficult to argue that the community in general has a right to demand compulsory immunisation from all members in the community. Individual immunisation offers a high level of protection from communicable disease and is readily available to the whole population. The risk of infection from an unimmunised child to an immunised individual will usually be very small. It seems, therefore, that the best option for people worried by the threat of infectious disease is to ensure that they themselves are immunised, rather than insisting on compulsory vaccination for all.

However, there are some groups who cannot be immunised. For example, they may be too young to receive immunisation or they may have another medical condition which prevents them from being immunised, such as leukaemia. These people are more at risk from unimmunised individuals.

On the whole, levels of population immunity or vaccine uptake are high in the UK for conditions where vaccination is available. For other diseases, poor access or non-availability of vaccination explain low levels of population immunity, rather than low levels of uptake.[18] If a small minority of parents decide not to have their children vaccinated, it is unlikely to alter significantly the level of population immunity and the chance of susceptible individuals contracting infectious disease. Because of this the community does not have a right to insist that all children are immunised, even to protect vulnerable persons.

However, the right of the community to be protected from infectious disease does seem to have some validity. The right seems to imply a duty on behalf of the health care system to offer immunisation to all those at risk of contracting communicable disease where a suitable, effective vaccine is available and the costs are not prohibitive.

What rights do children have?

Children do not necessarily have rights to health care in all circumstances, if treatments are of dubious effectiveness or are very expensive. However, it seems reasonable that they have a right to vaccination, if the danger of a severe infection is great and a safe vaccine is available (so that the chances of benefit to the children greatly outweigh the chances of harm). It seems that this right outweighs any rights parents have to choose. Social services have statutory legal powers to organise such vaccinations through the courts.

However, most immunisations given to children in the UK do not show benefits of such magnitude. This is because, in the UK, most vaccine-preventable infectious diseases have become rarer and there is a significant degree of population immunity, lessening the chances of children contracting them. In these cases, it becomes much more difficult to decide whose rights are overriding, parents' or children's.

If a child is due to receive an immunisation where the benefits to the child could be *significant* but not immediately life-saving and the parent has repeatedly not replied to the request for consent and is not present, the immunisation cannot go ahead because of the current legal position. This situation might occur when a child is in foster care.

Non-vaccination will increase the risk of serious infectious disease, but the increase is difficult to quantify. In contrast, most immunisations are procedures of very low risk. Generally, parents attach great importance to being involved in the decision-making process for immunisation of their child[19] but *may* accept the results of immunisation even if they were not present and have not given consent. For example, they might be the parents of children who are inadvertently immunised in mass campaigns. In view of these considerations, immunisation might sometimes be justified if the benefits, as so far known, outweigh the likely harm. More research is needed into the opinions of parents who repeatedly fail to give consent for the vaccination of their child and the quantification of risks and benefits for the child. If a majority of such parents were to object strongly, or the benefit to an individual child was small, the decision might need to be reversed.

Conclusion

In this chapter, the issue of whether there should be a compulsory vaccination programme has been discussed. In particular, it has concentrated on the dilemmas health care workers face when they decide whether it is morally justifiable to vaccinate a child where parental permission is refused or problematic.

Health care workers cannot justify compulsory immunisation for children against parents' wishes, purely in terms of the consequences that their actions yield. Parents can be wronged if their wishes are ignored and *usually* their wishes should be considered overriding. However, if children are considered to be in danger of being harmed *significantly*, their well-being is the primary concern.

174

Health care workers' decisions whether or not to consider parents' views as overriding, should be based on consideration of the respective rights of parents and children, namely parents' rights to rear their child according to their own standards and the children's rights to health care. Children's rights to health care include at least the right of access for vaccinations that prevent otherwise inevitably fatal diseases. Parents must maintain a minimal level of care for their children to earn their rights to rear according to their own standards.

If children are suspected of having a potentially fatal condition preventable by vaccination, such as rabies, and consent has been requested without reply, the immunisations should go ahead even if legal action might be needed to do this.

However it is not easy to argue that a child has a right to a vaccination when the balance of harms and risks is less obvious. Generally a child who is assumed to be well should not be immunised if the parent has refused, as the parent could be wronged. This is the case for most vaccinations in the UK, where protection is given for diseases which are not very prevalent or where there is already a high degree of population immunity.

In conclusion, it seems that a policy of compulsory vaccination cannot be justified, as the present system of non-compulsory vaccination promotes high levels of population immunity. However, if the level of population immunity were to fall for a particular vaccine-preventable infectious disease, compulsory vaccination might become a morally justifiable option.

Notes

I thank the *Journal of Medical Ethics* for permission to reproduce here, slightly adapted, the article published in the August 1999 issue.

1 Salisbury, D. M. and Begg, N. T., eds, *1996 Immunisation against Infectious Disease*, London: HMSO, 1996, inside cover.

2 Calman, K., *From the Chief Medical Officer: Measles, Mumps, Rubella (MMR) Vaccine, Chron's Disease and Austin*, London: Department of Health, 1998, pp. 1–4.

3 Donaldson, R. J., Donaldson, L. J., *Essential Public Health Medicine*, London: Kluwer Academic Publishers, 1993, p. 454.

4 See Salisbury and Begg, *1996 Immunisation*, p. 69.

5 Calman, K., *From the Chief Medical Officer: National Measles and, Rubella Immunisation Campaign*, London: Department of Health, 1994, pp. 1–5.

6 See Salisbury and Begg, *1996 Immunisation*, p. 7.

7 Ibid., p. 186.
8 Department of Health, *Children Act*, Part V, ch. 41, London: HMSO, 1989.
9 Beauchamp, T. L. and Childress, J. F., *Principles of Biomedical Ethics*, Oxford: Oxford University Press, 1994, pp. 69–85.
10 Hart, H. L. A., 'Are there any natural rights?', in J. Waldon, ed., *Theories of Rights*, Oxford: Oxford University Press, 1984, p. 79.
11 Mill, J. S., 'On moral obligation and justice', in *Utilitariansim*, ed. H. B. Acton, London: Dent and Sons, 1972, pp. 40–2.
12 Buchanan, A. E. and Brock, D. W., *Deciding for Others: The Ethics of Surrogate Decision Making*, Cambridge: Cambirdge University Press, 1989, pp. 230–6. Dworkin, G. *The Theory and Practice of Autonomy*, Cambridge: Cambridge University Press, 1988, pp. 89–103. Koocher, G. P., Keith-Speigel, P. C., *Children, Ethics and the Law*, Lincoln: University of Nebraska press, 1990, p. 13. Brazier, M. *Medicine, Patients and the Law*, Harmondsworth: Penguin Books, 1992, p. 95.
13 Archard, D. *Children, Rights and Childhood*, London: Routledge, 1993, pp. 104–30. Buchanan and Brock, *Deciding for Others*, pp. 230–6.
14 Dworkin, *Theory and Practice of Autonomy*, pp. 89–103.
15 Archard, *Children, Rights and Childhood*, pp. 104–30.
16 See Salisbury and Begg, *1996 Immunisation*, pp. 159–60.
17 Holder, A., *Legal Issues in Paediatric and Adolescent Medicine*, New Haven, Conn.: Yale University Press, 1985, pp. 102–9. Bainham, A. with Creaney, S., *Children: The Modern Law*, Jordan, 1993, p. 93.
18 See Archard, *Children, Rights and Childhood*, p. 10.
19 See Salisbury and Begg, *1996 Immunisation*, p. 7.

14

ETHICAL ISSUES IN DENTAL SCREENING AND SURVEYING OF SCHOOLCHILDREN

Nigel Monaghan

This chapter examines legal and ethical issues regarding consent for dental screening and surveying of schoolchildren. These examinations can be conducted without positive parental consent. Reasons for this are covered. Practical approaches which seek both to inform and to minimise harm are proposed.

Why are school dental examinations conducted?

Tooth decay is still a common disease. Over 40 per cent of 5-year-olds in England have experienced tooth decay and over 35 per cent have untreated decay in one or more of their teeth. During the school year 1995/6, 172,659 5-year-old children across the United Kingdom underwent, in school, a survey examination of their teeth.[1] In the same year 2,829,209 schoolchildren aged 5–15 underwent, in school, a screening examination of their teeth in England alone.[2] The examinations are conducted in schools because they afford easy access to almost all children. Examinations conducted in schools are also inexpensive compared with home-based examinations. The examinations consist of a visual examination of teeth using a light and mirror with use of a dental probe to remove debris from obscured surfaces. Fresh clean instruments are used for each child.

School dental screening

All children should be offered a screening at least three times during their school life.[3] The aim is to identify decay at an early stage. It is believed that early identification of tooth decay should result in smaller fillings, avoidance of need for extraction and an opportunity to deliver prevention. These preventive measures and care are targeted at individuals known to be at risk from decay. The screening is offered to benefit the health of the child's teeth.

These examinations have been regularly conducted in all state schools from 1944 until the present day, by the school dental service until 1977 and the community dental service since then. The proportion of children examined is high (over 94 per cent of target screening numbers in England in 1995/6). In part this may be explained by the law covering such examinations, which does not require positive parental consent. This matter is considered further below.

The high proportion of children examined is in contrast to the lower proportion (68 per cent) of those under 18 who are registered with a dentist.[4] Unlike registration with a medical practitioner, registration with a dentist lapses after 15 months unless renewed by the patient. The levels of registration at population level appear to be relatively static although many individuals drift in and out of registration.[5] Often there is a stimulus such as toothache which prompts attendance of those not registered. Toothache occurs at an advanced stage of the decay of teeth.

In the United Kingdom in the 1990s tooth decay is associated with deprivation.[6] In deprived areas a larger proportion of children have decay and those with decay each have a greater number of teeth affected by decay.[7] These are the children whose parents are least likely to respond to a letter requesting permission for a dental examination.

In summary:

- Dental decay is a very common disease in children.
- Many children are not registered with a dentist.
- Many children do not attend a dentist until they experience problems associated with advanced decay.
- It is believed that early diagnosis will help to save teeth from the effects of tooth decay.
- Schools offer easy and inexpensive access to the majority of children including many who are not otherwise in contact with a dentist.
- Tooth decay is associated with deprivation.
- Parents of children living in deprived areas are less likely to respond to forms sent to them.

School dental survey

Dental surveys of schoolchildren provide local and national information on the health of teeth. The primary aim of the survey is to obtain information for planning purposes, and therefore the survey is conducted for the benefit of the whole community. The child may benefit from the use of that information, but no direct health gain is anticipated. The survey examination may be conducted together with, or separated from, a screening examination. When survey and screening are conducted together the teeth are often examined twice, using different criteria.

By using information from surveys, sites with high levels of disease can be targeted for health promotion work. Schools with low disease levels can be identified and the frequency of screening there can be reduced. When linked with other data, such as deprivation scores, the information can help with understanding of patterns of disease. Such evidence helps to justify additional funding for preventive or care services. Data from surveys can also be used to evaluate whether interventions are improving the health of teeth.

For survey information to be free from bias (and therefore meaningful) it is important that a high proportion of the children sampled are examined. If a significant proportion of a survey sample are lost then the findings may not be representative of the wider population. Children and parents cannot be forced to permit an examination; legally, this would be assault. However specific legislation facilitates a high examination rate by permitting examination of children whose parents have not refused.

In summary:

- The survey is conducted for the benefit of the whole community.
- It is important that almost every child in the sample is examined.

The legal basis of school dental (and medical) inspections

Legislation imposes a duty to inspect the teeth of children in schools. The 1977 National Health Service Act s 5 (as amended by the Health and Medicines Act 1988 s 10) requires the dental inspection of pupils at appropriate intervals. No explanation of the purpose of the dental inspection is made in the Act. It would appear reasonable to interpret this term to cover both dental screenings and dental surveys.

In each case the nature of the process is the same: visual examination of the teeth. It is the purpose of the examination that differs. The word examination will be used hereafter in referring to dental 'inspections'.

Education authorities are required to encourage dental examinations. The 1996 Education Act s 520 (2) imposes on local education authorities a duty to encourage and assist pupils to take advantage of the medical and dental examinations and treatment they are under a duty to offer. Section 536 (2) of the same Act imposes a similar duty on grant maintained schools:

> Provided that if the parent of any pupil gives . . . notice that he objects . . . the pupil shall not be encouraged or assisted so to do.

This law relating to school-based medical and dental examinations is unusual. Section 520 (2) and 536 (2) also apply to treatment in the school setting (e.g. vaccinations) although 'negative consent' is now rarely used for this purpose. Indeed guidance for medical (as opposed to dental) examinations, which may include undressing children or genital examinations, suggests that positive parental consent should be obtained.[8]

This law has been in existence since the 1944 Education Act came into force. The custom and practice of most community dental services has been to send a note to parents indicating that a dental inspection will take place shortly without or, more commonly these days, with an indication that the parent can refuse. Children are then examined unless a parental refusal has been notified. Clearly parents may not receive letters, or be unable to read or understand them. Responses may not be delivered. In these cases children who co-operate will be examined even though no positive consent has been given. The law which permits this is statutory law (made by Parliament). Most law on consent is common law (judge-made law which has evolved over hundreds of years); statutory law overrides common law.

The approach of notifying parents by letter sent from the school and examining those children whose parents have not refused is commonly termed 'negative consent' by those using it. Strictly speaking consent has not been given, although an examination would appear to be permissible within the law because of the provisions of the 1996 Education Act.

Features of consent

A valid consent has three features, it is:

- adequately informed;
- voluntarily given;
- given by an individual with capacity to consent.[9]

Consent acts in two ways. It protects the doctor or dentist from litigation and it respects self-determination of the patient. As proposed in a court judgement,

> Every human being of adult years and sound mind has a right to determine what shall be done with his own body; and a surgeon who performs an operation without his patient's consent, commits an assault.[10]

Consent is not a process, it is 'a state of mind of the patient which respects the legal and ethical right of the patient' to decide what is done to them. Patients need information on the nature and purpose of what is proposed.[11] They also require information on material risks.[12]

In ethical terms the law is attempting to protect patients from harm, and balance health care's potential for benefit (assuming that medical care does benefit patients) against patients' right to choose their own health care (respecting their autonomy).

Consent and children

The law recognises that young children lack the necessary intelligence and understanding to make decisions about what is done to them.[13] It permits others who have the care of the child to decide on their behalf. In a judgement in 1992, Lord Donaldson likened consent to a flak jacket[14] (a defensive medicine view of consent). He stated that a doctor needs only one consent to protect him from suit for assault. There are a number of potential sources of consent for dental examination of a child in a school setting:

- either parent;
- a child aged 16 or 17;
- a teacher who has the care of the child;
- a 'Gillick competent' child aged under 16 (see below for the Gillick case).

Parents have long had a right to consent based on the common law. A teacher who has the care of a child may 'do what is reasonable in the circumstances of the case for safeguarding or promoting the child's welfare'.[15] Interestingly this would cover a screening examination but not a survey, since only the former is intended to be for the benefit of the child.

Since 1969, when the Family Law Reform Act came into force, children aged 16 or 17 have been able to consent to medical treatment or diagnostic procedures. Interestingly, children aged 16 or 17 cannot refuse treatment when a valid consent is given by another who has the authority to give consent, such as a parent.[16] Such a refusal is, however, a very important consideration for clinicians making decisions and for others considering giving consent.[17]

The Gillick case considered contraception for girls aged under 16 without parental consent.[18] The judgement was made on general principles and would therefore be applicable to other areas of medical treatment.[19] It established that children under 16 have a right to consent to medical and dental treatments when they have sufficient intelligence and understanding to be capable of making up their own minds. This judgement has been reinforced and supplemented by the Children Act s 48 (3), which states that children with sufficient understanding can 'make an informed decision to refuse to submit to a medical or psychiatric examination or other assessment'. The decision on whether a child has sufficient intelligence and understanding is a matter of judgement for the doctor or dentist. The law, however, gives no further guidance on how this should be tested.

Ethical implications of the legal framework

Use of negative consent promotes the uptake of dental examinations; it promotes the assumed greater good to either the community (for surveys) or the individual (for screening). The 1944 Education Act acknowledges that some parents may not want their children to be examined and allows them to refuse; it respects a decision made by a parent for the child's welfare.

There is a price paid for this promotion of greater good. Some children may be examined against their parents' wishes because their parents did not have an opportunity to refuse. Some parents may make a decision even though they might have wanted more information before deciding. Opportunities to ask questions are limited if using letters sent home from school. Since 1944 there have been many changes in consent law related to disclosure of information and to medical treatment of children. These may have been reflected in the practice of some community dental services, but they are not incorporated into the 1944 Act.

Modern law on consent identifies a number of potential sources of consent. Differences of opinion could result in one party refusing and another consenting. The decision on how to act in these circumstances should be made on ethical grounds.

Ethical dilemmas in school dental surveys and screenings

Commonly recognised ethical principles in medical and dental care are those of non-maleficence (doing no harm), beneficence (promotion of benefit) and respect for autonomy (respecting a person's choice and ability to choose). Sometimes it is unclear in ethical terms which principle carries most weight.[20] There are a number of complicating factors that must be considered when attempting to strike the right balance between benefit, harm and respecting individuals' views.

Informing parents and children

The 1996 Act protects the dentist from litigation and encourages an examination intended to benefit the child. It does not require parents to be informed nor parental consent to be obtained, but rather requires that any parental objection is respected. Therefore the law does not promote parental decision-making, but it does promote respecting a parent's decision. Common law on consent requires information on the nature and purpose of what is proposed and on material risks. There is no indication of the volume of information to be given to parents when using negative consent, but to make an informed decision parents need the same type of information whether 'negative' or positive consent is used. Parents should also know that they have a right to refuse and how to do so if they are to have an opportunity to refuse. Community dental services would be well advised to ensure that the letters they send home contain the same type of information required for positive written consent. This will ensure that they are doing all they can to respect parental choice. Such an approach is not only good legal practice, it is good ethical practice.

Children should be informed too. The United Kingdom has adopted the United Nations Convention on the Rights of the Child. This states that children who are capable of forming their own views have the right to express those views freely and that these views should be given due weight in accordance with the age and maturity of the child.[21] An underlying principles of the Children Act 1989 is that children should be kept informed about what happens to them and should participate when decisions are made about their future. Use of 'negative consent' does little to inform children before assessing their co-operation. It may conform to the Convention, but it does not inform them. If we are serious about respecting autonomy then we must include informing children.

Children, parents and schools

The law promotes the child's best interests by encouraging an examination. However there are three parties on the receiving end of a school dental examination; children, parents and schools. These parties may have priorities other than promoting the health of the teeth of the child. For the school, education is the primary concern. There is an existing relationship between parents and schools and it is in the interests of the education and future employment prospects of the child that this relationship is not harmed.

As children age they become more responsible and the law gives them increasing control over their lives.[22] Children do not always agree with decisions made on their behalf by their parents. And indeed parents may disagree with each other.

Relationships involving schools

Recent changes in the law on consent recognise that some children could consent to aspects of medical and dental care before the age of 16. Community dentists are occasionally faced with a child who asks for his or her teeth to be examined and a parental refusal for such an examination. It is not in the best interests of the child for a dental examination to generate friction that damages the relationship between parents and schools. If a parent was unhappy that the child had been examined and blamed the school the parent could withdraw the child from the school, with potential harm to the child's education. A child should only be examined if the dentist is certain that the benefit of an examination would outweigh potential harm to the parent–school relationship.

Schools may wish to protect their relationship with parents. In response to a parental complaint the school could make it difficult or impossible for the community dental service to conduct future examination of children's teeth. This is contrary to the interests of other children who might benefit from a screening and the community who benefit from survey work. Clearly the community dentists must be aware of the need to protect these relationships. Therefore any indication of parental refusal should be accepted at face value and respected, even one verbally delivered by the child. The legislation states that a child can be examined provided the parent has not notified a refusal. It does not state how that refusal should be delivered.

Parent–child conflict

Potential conflict between the desires of parents and children presents problems that can be defused by considered responses. If notice has been given that a parent does not want his or her child examined then this should normally be respected, even when the child requests an examination. The examination is unlikely to uncover anything serious and urgent to the child's short-term health and no treatment can be given immediately, in the absence of suitable equipment. One way to resolve the conflict would be to ask the child to discuss his or her wishes with the parent(s).

In the reverse situation a forced examination may cause more harm than good. As letters used to inform parents do not state that uncooperative children will be examined against their will, an examining dentist would be well advised not to examine the child. Rather the dentist should inform the parents of the non-examination of the child so that they can make other arrangements.

Parent–parent conflict

Parents can disagree. Here it should be remembered that 'negative consent' is not a true form of consent, and as statutory law it overrides common law. Thus if one parent objects to the examination then the child cannot be examined using 'negative consent' even if the other parent agrees. Positive written consent of the agreeing parent would be one way to resolve this problem, although it could still cause problems for the school with the refusing parent. An alternative would be to write to the agreeing parent explaining that the examination could not be conducted because an objection had been made by the other parent and to suggest that the agreeing parent should make other arrangements for a dental examination outside the school setting.

Promoting greater good and retaining freedom of choice

There are a number of potential sources of consent for these examinations. As dental survey and screening examinations involve children as young as 5 it is not possible to turn to children as the only potential source of consent. On the other hand if parents were used as a source of positive written consent then the wishes of the child would not be involved in the decision process. Also, many children would not participate because parents did not take the trouble to complete and return a form. This would seriously undermine the surveys and exclude many of the most needy children from the screening process. Although teachers are theoretically a source of consent for a screening examination, using school staff as a 'flak jacket' is not recommended as this may harm relationships involving the school. As a statute exists which permits examination of children provided parents have not refused it would seem wise to continue to use it provided:

- Parents are informed about the nature and purpose of the intended examination.
- The explanation is given in simple language.
- Any material risks are mentioned (for a simple dental examination there are no material risks).
- Parents are told that unless they indicate a refusal their child will be examined.
- Parents should be told how to refuse.

This type of approach will give parents the opportunity to make an informed decision. It has been used in the Trent Region of the NHS (South Yorkshire and most of the East Midlands) with little impact on refusal rates.[23] This approach gives more respect to parental decision-making, but does not inform the children involved.

Ethically, an explanation should be given to children of all ages in language they can understand; this respects them as persons. Legally, it conforms to the requirements of the Children Act. While many 5-year-olds may not be able to consent to a simple dental examination, many children over 10 should be capable of doing so. To make an informed decision children require information (and an opportunity to ask questions). A simple way to deliver this is to speak to a class of schoolchildren. An explanation of what is proposed and why (the nature and purpose) including any material risks will be sufficient to allow many children to make an informed choice. Examination of co-operating children of sufficient maturity would generate a legally valid consent and respect their ability to make such a decision. If children have insufficient maturity to make a decision, but do co-operate, they will have been involved in the decision-making as much as they can be.

There is no reason why the giving of information to children as suggested above should not be combined with use of 'negative consent'. Children of parents who have not refused can be given an appropriate explanation. This approach respects parental refusal, but also informs children and involves them in the decision process.

A further modification of 'negative consent' is possible: school entry consent. Normally consent is required on each occasion care is delivered. Consent to a previous examination does not give a doctor or dentist a right to examine again and again. But the 1996 Act does allow medical and dental examination and treatment in a school setting provided parents have not refused. If a school entry positive consent form were used this could be renewed by means of a letter sent to parents prior to each school dental examination, giving them a fresh opportunity to refuse. This approach may add legal weight to the defence of a dentist or doctor, but it is not clear that it respects the autonomy of parents any more than use of a positive consent form or better informed negative consent.

Summary

Currently information given to parents and to children is often extremely limited. If parents are to make informed decisions and children are to be involved in the decision process then they should in future be given more information. This information can be given by modifying current practice without major impact on examination rates.

Given the number of potential sources of consent for examination of children and a statute that permits examination provided parents have not objected, there is great potential for misunderstanding by dentists, doctors, parents, schools and children. This mis-understanding could damage relationships between these parties. Consideration should be given to the wider best interests of the child when resolving dilemmas created by these complex issues.

Notes

1 N. B. Pitts and D. J. Evans (1997) 'The dental caries experience of 5-year-old children in the United Kingdom', Surveys coordinated by the British Association for the Study of Community Dentistry in 1995/6, *Community Dental Health* 14, pp. 47–52.

2 Data provided by Department of Health.

3 Department of Health (1997) *Primary Dental Care Services*, HSG (97) 4.

4 Dental Practice Board (1997) Registrations: GDS Quarterly Statistics October–December 1997.

5 J. A. Davies, Z. J. Nugent, N. B. Pitts and P. A. Smith (1998) 'A longitudinal study of the dental care of adults in the general dental service in Scotland: the first 6 years, 1988–1994', *British Dental Journal* 184(2), pp. 85–9.

6 C. Jones, G. Taylor, K. Woods, G. Whittle, D. Evans and P. Young (1997) 'Jarman underprivileged area scores, tooth decay and the effect of water fluoridation', *COmmunity Dental Health* 14(3), pp. 156–60.

7 N. Monaghan and R. Heesterman (1999) 'Dental caries, social deprivation and enhanced capitation for children', *British Dental Journal* 186, pp. 238–40.

8 NHS Executive (1996) *Child Health in the Community: A Guide to Good Practice*, London: Department of Health, pp. 45–53.

9 I. Kennedy and A. Grubb (1994) *Medical Law: Text with Materials*, 2nd edn, London: Butterworths, p. 104.

10 *Schloendorff* v. *Society of New York Hospital* (1914) 211 NY 125 and 126.

11 *Chatterton* v. *Gerson* [1981] 1 All ER 257; (1980) 1 BMLR 80.

12 *Sidaway* v. *Governors of Royal Bethlem Hospital* [1984] AC 871 (1985) 1 BMLR 132 1 All ER 643 (HL).

13 *Gillick* v. *West Norfolk and Wisbech Area Health Authority* [1986] AC 112, [1985] 3 All ER 402; (1985) 2 BMLR 11.

14 *Re W (a minor) (medical treatment)* [1992] 4 All ER 627 per Lord Donaldson at p. 635.

15 Children Act 1989 s 3 (5).

16 *Re W (a minor) (medical treatment)* [1992] 4 All ER 627.

17 *Re W (a minor) (medical treatment)* [1992] 4 All ER 627.

18 *Gillick* v. *West Norfolk and Wisbech Area Health Authority* [1986] AC 112, [1985] 3 All ER 402; (1985) 2 BMLR 11.

19 M. Brazier (1992) 'Doctors and child patients', in *Medicine, Patients and the Law*, London: Penguin Books.

20 T. L. Beauchamp and J. F. Childress (1989) 'Types of ethical theory', in *Principles of Biomedical Ethics*, 3rd edn, New York: Oxford University Press.

21 United Nations Convention on the Rights of the Child (1992) Article 12, London: HMSO.

22 Children Act 1989 s 48 (3).

23 N. Monaghan (in preparation) 'Parents need more information: an audit of more informed use of negative consent', *Community Dental Health*.

INDEX